Buc
Tal
Modern Times
Stories of the Soul

By the same author

Buddhist
Tales in Modern Times
Stories of the Soul

Ven Gyomyo Nakamura

STERLING PAPERBACKS
An imprint of
Sterling Publishers (P) Ltd.
A-59, Okhla Industrial Area, Phase-II,
New Delhi-110020.
Tel: 26387070, 26386209; Fax: 91-11-26383788
E-mail: mail@sterlingpublishers.com
www.sterlingpublishers.com

Buddhist Tales in Modern Times: Stories of the Soul
© 2013, Ven Gyomyo Nakamura
ISBN 978 81 207 8527 4
First Edition 2009
Second Edition (Revised) 2013

Translated by **Ven. Shakya Indrajala**
Line drawings by **Ven. Thupstan Paldan**
Edited by **Upendra Kumar and Sandeep Kumar Pandey**
Research Scholars, CRS, JNU, New Delhi

All rights are reserved.
No part of this publication may be reproduced, stored in a retrieval system or transmitted, in any form or by any means, mechanical, photocopying, recording or otherwise, without prior written permission of the original publisher.

Printed in India
Printed and Published by **Sterling Publishers Pvt. Ltd.,**
New Delhi-110 020.

Contents

	Acknowledgements	6
1.	The Old Amchi	7
2.	Chunzhung the Little Lama	18
3.	Simple Sonam	24
4.	King Yak	32
5.	Kuro	39
6.	The Big Tree	43
7.	Kumari	47
8.	Tenzin	54
9.	The Little Bird	58
10.	The Donkey's Pilgrimage	86

Acknowledgements

I am immensely grateful to Mrs. Suzie Shubber, Ms Zaki Shubber, Ms Yasmin Shubber, and Ven. Thupstan Paldan for their support.

1

The Old Amchi

The word "Amchi" is a Tibetan word. It means a doctor who practises Tibetan medicine, which has been passed down for generations.

The Tibetan plateau sees India to the south of the Himalayas, China to the north and the Silk Road to the west with the Middle Eastern countries beyond, through which caravans have come and gone since ancient times. Tibetan medicine was born from the mixing of Chinese medicine, Indian Ayurveda, Middle Eastern, Unani and Buddhism.

The Old Amchi was a doctor of Tibetan medicine. He cured the illnesses of people in the village and healed their hearts. His son Dorje had been sent to school and become a doctor of Western medicine. He worked in the hospital in town.

Horses became cars.

Lamps became light bulbs.

Evening prayers became television.

Ethnic clothes became Western attire.

This notable family, which had carried on a tradition of Tibetan medicine for generations, likewise had been amchis, but became doctors.

Recently the Old Amchi had come to often idly bask in the sun, gazing towards the Himalayas under a clear blue sky while recollecting old times.

Everyone probably knows about the placebo effect, right?

The placebo effect is where, even in Western medicine, the doctor gives fake medicine to the patient and says, "This is really good medicine!" When they get them to take it for a bit, they strangely recover from their illness. It might look like they are somehow deceiving the patient like it was fraud, which is why they study it as a form of knowledge and don't speak of it to keep it away from people.

The Old Amchi himself didn't know that half his medical practice, which he had done throughout a lifetime, was believed to be the placebo effect as it was called in Western medicine.

He would diligently walk around the Himalayas looking for herbs to use as medicine. He would diligently recite sutras while mixing the herbs with spices in a stone bowl before placing them for several weeks before the Buddha as an offering and wholeheartedly praying. When a patient came, he would listen to their complaints and pray together with them. He offered advice on lifestyle choices. He would take their pulse, feeling the murmur of the flowing stream within the body, and then prepare the appropriate medicine.

He thought that when the effect of the medicine, his own prayers and the feeling of belief on the part of the patient came together, it all became a kind of light of the Buddha's compassion which enveloped the person and healed the illnesses of their mind and body.

That's why he thought he was just assisting the patient in healing themselves through the Buddha.

Horses became cars.

Lanterns became light bulbs.

Evening prayers became television.

Like ethnic clothes becoming Western attire, his son Dorje also became an outstanding doctor.

Life was becoming easy and prosperous, and he was looked after by his faithful son Dorje with everyday a blessing, but, although it couldn't really be said, he couldn't help but wonder if something had been lost in his house, the village and town.

The Old Amchi came to suffer poor vision and his son carried out some surgery on him at the hospital. He recovered his vision. People who had suffered great burns were also treated at the hospital and recovered. Even those people who could only seemingly throw themselves at the mercy of the Buddha and pray, recovered and were discharged from the hospital. Still, it felt like the hospital was such a lonely place.

In such a strange sterile environment with bleak white walls, and white clad doctors and nurses, it felt like even healthy people would get ill.

He felt it was like being in a factory. He saw how everyone lined up and then had their five minute diagnosis before getting a prescription from the chemist with their slip of paper and then going home.

For the Old Amchi, his eyes had been given to him so he could hang beautiful Thangka paintings. His nose had been given so he could light incense as medicine. His ears had been given so he could recite sutras along with bells and drums. His voice had been given so he could recite sutras with his patients. He would listen to the murmurs of the ten streams deep within the body. He could then provide medicine and treatment.

This is why until now he never thought that "life is good" and "death is bad". To him life was the start of death and death was the entrance to life. Health was given to us and illness was training for the mind. He never thought one had to somehow live no matter what.

One day when he went to meet his son at the hospital, he heard his son speak to a family. Lying on the bed was a critically ill and unconscious old man with a tube up his nose and his heart rate being monitored. His son was saying, "He still has two weeks!"

However, as he himself was aware, he had been able to see again through eye surgery and was being supported with a stipend from his son; he could not say anything and was just left disheartened.

In the old days many rich patients would give him money. He might not have received any money from poor farmers, but instead he received vegetables and wheat. Now the rich people flew to the city hospital in a plane, and it was nothing but the poor elderly visiting him.

One day a group of doctors on an inspection tour from Western countries came to Dorje's hospital. Dorje, who had been assigned to look after the large group of famous doctors by the chief physician, did his best to explain the local situation and hospital and play a good host.

However, it had all been written in the report from the government and while touring the hospital the leader of the group suddenly said, "Actually, everyone is interested in Tibetan medicine, so could you possibly introduce a Tibetan doctor?"

Dorje promptly replied, "Actually, in this town it is only my father who carries on the Tibetan medicine tradition. Please come tomorrow. I'll introduce him at lunch."

Dorje immediately set about getting the meal prepared and explained to his father how great these doctors were. The Old Amchi thought he shouldn't embarrass his son. The night before he was worried and couldn't sleep.

However, the following day when the group of blue-eyed doctors came, the guests all treated him as if he were an eminent master of a temple, sitting around him in a circle and asking questions despite the day before Dorje having told him not to offend them.

Their questions were the same doubts as the Old Amchi had held for the longest time about Western medicine.

The Old Amchi was increasingly enveloped in a warm light and he started speaking of all that he had acquired in life, the wisdom that had been transmitted from his ancestors from generation to generation, and the great

knowledge that came with understanding the medical system that had been successively conveyed all the way from the Buddha's personal physician Jivaka.

His son had been translating without thinking anything when in the middle of it he felt as if the Buddha and his ancestors were speaking to him through his father, whereupon he started translating earnestly.

While Dorje had seriously studied Western medicine, and was now in front of the Western doctors he deeply respected, he knew nothing of the medical wisdom his father, the one closest to him, possessed. At the same time he came to quickly feel ashamed of himself for having looked down on his father, who now seemed to glow like a Bodhisattva.

The talk did not end in one day. It lasted three days from morning to evening.

The Old Amchi intuitively felt that he had received a chance, thanks to the Buddha, to convey all his life experiences and spiritual legacy to his son Dorje while these messengers were visiting from the Western countries.

For three days he used all his strength to explain everything.

The group of doctors were delighted and paid their respects to the Amchi's family. Before leaving they said, "In the future this will become a spiritual support for medicine."

A bit later in the early morning the Old Amchi did three full body-length prostrations on the floor before the Buddha and then recited some sutras before taking his last breath. He was eighty years old.

Dorje in the presence of his father, who had never burdened his family nor become ill while living a fulfilling life, realized the idea of "life is the start of death and death is the entrance to rebirth" despite having thought "life is good, death is bad".

Indeed, Dorje had inherited the successive legacy of Tibetan medicine from his ancestors.

Thanks to having been able to study Western medicine, his father's wisdom had been conveyed through that group of Western doctors.

Just as the ancient Tibetans had taken the essences of Chinese medicine from the north, Ayurveda from the south and Unani from the west and created Tibetan medicine, Dorje now had started a completely new form of Buddhism by also taking in the wisdom of Western medicine.

Just as the once nomadic Tibetans had not rejected the surrounding cultural traditions around them while accepting them all into a kind of work of art suitable for Tibet, Dorje now had started to make a work of art in his mind with the wisdom his father had given him and Western medicine. Up until now he had thought his father's job was different from his. He felt he had been supporting him because his father never received a pension. He realized that in actuality it was through his parents that he had been living in the great radiance of the Buddha's compassion.

He also came to know that he had inherited a precious legacy.

In the meanwhile, he stopped driving and started walking to the hospital.

He turned off the light bulbs and instead used a lamp as an offering to the Buddha.

He turned off the television and made time for prayers.

He stopped wearing Western clothes and started wearing Tibetan clothes.

After returning home from the hospital in the evening he would start his Tibetan medicine practice at home. Everyone started calling him the Amchi Doctor.

The borders between Western and Tibetan medicine were gone.

Following the industrial revolution everyone had specialist jobs, and everything changed with the arrival of aeroplanes, mobile phones, Internet and satellite television.

A new civilization had started in the mind of Dorje on the Tibetan plateau.

After the forty-nine day service for his father had ended, Dorje truly believed his father, who had spent three days talking to the Western doctors about his own experiences, would follow his calling and be reborn in a faraway Western country. He also knew that his reborn father would come here in twenty to thirty years, whereupon he who had studied Western medicine would share his experiences just as his father had.

The tradition did not end as a tradition, but became a kind of special medicine which would continue onward into the next life. The murmur of the great river could be heard.

Dorje then pressed his palms together towards the evening sky and prayed for his father's liberation before returning to the treatment room where he smiled at the patients from around the world who had gathered. He went back to work, lending his ear to hear the pains of their mind and body, and listening to the murmurs of the flowing streams in the body.

This was a family tradition that had been passed down through the generations to Dorje. His daytime job at the hospital was the modern medicine.

Forms and figures change, but what flows to the roots is the always unchanging brilliant light of the Buddha's compassion. That light changes form throughout time, helping many people. When you have a mind that is at ease and not bothered by things, then you can see how that compassion and those practices exist through time.

To know this is to know the mind of the Old Amchi and the change of mind that Dorje experienced.

Around you there are people who practice the Bodhisattva path without anyone knowing. They do unexpected professions and are unexpected people.

Whether you believe in them or not, they work so that all sentient beings can attain enlightenment and become Buddhas themselves. The promise of the Buddha carries onward like a stream, enriching people as it goes along.

You should quietly listen for the sound of that murmur of the river.

That stream within the spirit will definitely answer.

What did the Western doctors ask the Old Amchi?

How did the Old Amchi reply?

You can probably together hear the murmur of that stream in the spirit.

That is the subtle sound of compassion and wisdom being conveyed from mind to mind.

Comment:

In this story I took a direct approach about the problem of life and death in Western and general medicine. As civilization advances it has become a time when people are living longer. When overcoming illness became the main concern, questions concerning our fate, the afterlife, liberation of the spirit, and religion as it exists after all the medicine and funerals got basically ignored.

Furthermore, the effects of natural and spiritual forms of healing have come to people's attention even in Japan which is now taking too much medicine and fully committed to Western medicine. In Tibet psychological processes are connected to faith, forming what is the unique system of Tibetan medicine. Today what is seemingly thought to be superstition might offer a kind of spiritual process in the face of the collapse of the Japanese health insurance system and the old age care which is increasing every year. This prompted me to write this story.

The Tibetans also still have a sense of believing in rebirth, much like what was the ancient Japanese attitude towards death, which is why I want to bring up said issues with modern Japanese people.

2

Chunzhung the Little Lama

In Tibetan a little monk in the temple is called *chunzhung*.

At a young age boys are made to live apart from other people in a temple that houses other monks where they study, pray, help out with various tasks like looking after the meals of the senior monks and cleaning. Over the years they are trained to become full monks. Even if they longed for their mothers and wanted to get into mischief, the *chunzhung* had to strictly be in isolation, study, pray and run around the temple doing chores. The dedication and sacrifice in them is admirable. They, eventually, become a spiritual support and pillar for their people.

Chunzhung Tsering was different from the other *chunzhung* in that he was an orphan. His mother and father had both died when he was very young, and the villagers had placed him in this temple. The other *chunzhung* would receive gifts from their parents and the parents visited them too. On days like these he would dash into the dimly lit main shrine hall and, unable to hold back the tears, he wept.

This is why he was called Crybaby Tsering. Some bigger monks pampered him, while the other little ones teased him. He became the temple mascot. It was a name he was given out of affection too and he grew to accept it.

He had lost his parents at a very young age, so he did not know how they looked like.

One day the master of the temple pointed to a golden Buddha statue and said, "This is your father."

He then pointed to an image of the feminine Tara and said, "This is your mother."

Having heard this from the master, Tsering truly believed it.

It helped him to accept their absence. Later, when the other *chunzhung* were meeting their parents, he would compare them in his mind to his own mother and father — the Buddha and Tara — and he no longer felt envious and stopped crying.

Tsering's only complaint was that his mother and father, the Buddha and Tara, always kept smiling, but never said anything to him. One day when everyone was fast asleep, he went into the shrine room and offered his prayers and spent some secret time in front of the dimly illuminated statue of Buddha.

Now, every day, late at night he had his secret time. In the beginning, he felt afraid of the dark and being alone in the shrine with the statues. He would be on the verge of crying. But then he thought how strange it was to be afraid of meeting your mother and father, and then it became part of his daily schedule.

He made a vow to visit them for a hundred days. He recalled that his master had said that a practice should be followed for at least hundred days.

During the daytime when he was not working he studied — reading and writing — with everyone. Along with learning how to read and write he could also read people's complexions and minds. He had an unfortunate childhood, but this was a rare power that he possessed. For ordinary people it was like a superpower.

Crybaby Tsering was strangely able to see into the minds of other *chunzhuns* when they were angry, crying, fighting, stumbling and falling over. Tsering could foresee things and so he did not ruffle any feathers.

He was called a sharp kid, but as he could read the minds of others, he did not exert himself more than he had to for most things. Thus, he could devote himself to prayer.

Several days passed, the Buddha and Tara still didn't speak to him, so he would just speak to them and update them on his daily life. As he did this, his feelings of sadness, pain and loneliness eased and he was able to sleep peacefully.

Finally, the hundredth day arrived. He had fulfilled his vow.

That night, Tsering was fast asleep and he dreamt of the Buddha. He was so radiant that Tsering couldn't open his eyes. In an encompassing voice the Buddha said, "You have done well, good child."

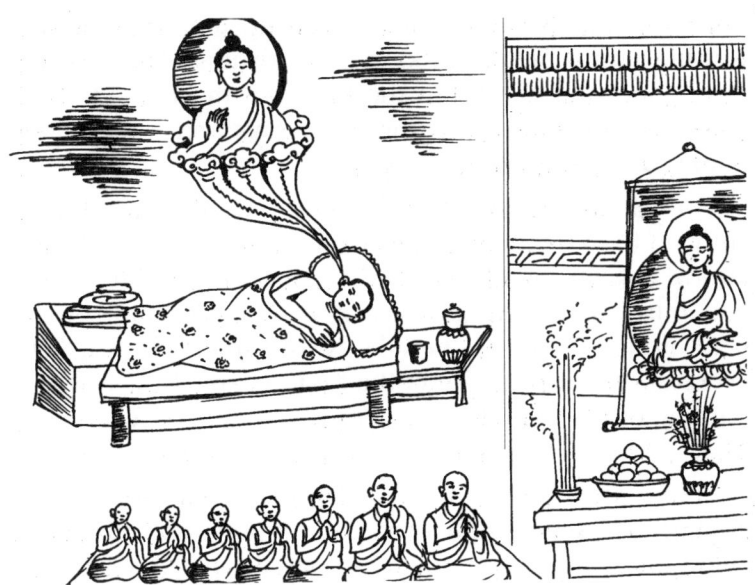

The image gradually changed into Tara, shifting from white to yellow, whereby Tsering could open his eyes and fix his sight on her form. She whispered to him, "Tsering, I will grant you just one wish as a reward for your dedicated practice."

Tara had many twin sisters of various other colours, so she could grant any wish it seemed. Tsering felt happy and proud to have such a mother. He gave it a sincere thought and then said, "Mom, I now have the ability to read minds. I want to be able to write minds so I can be a kid who can both read and write."

Tara laughed and nodded. "Well, well, you've become a good child. You will have a hard time, but I will grant you your wish."

She then disappeared into the cosmos.

Soon a time came a that the temple was in frenzy. The adorable little Crybaby Tsering was on the verge of dying with a high fever and faint breath. The doctor had left hopeless and the monks had given up too. They started reciting sutras while striking their drums. They recited throughout the night, but the faint breath lingered. They continued reciting sutras for three days and three nights hoping for a miracle to happen.

In the early morning of the third day, Tsering's breath stopped for a moment and he opened his eyes wide before taking a deep breath. He had recovered. The high fever had burnt away the poisons of body and mind, giving new life to a beautiful new body and mind. Tsering told everyone about having met the Buddha and Tara, but said nothing of his last wish. Everyone strangely believed him. They told him that they had been reciting Tara's sutra.

From that day onwards, Tsering went from being a sharp kid who could read complexions and minds to being one who could also write down what those minds were thinking. As a holy child, who could heal the pains in the hearts of people, Tsering became very important to the temple and people from all over the country came to see him.

People in the temple also learnt that late at night he would prostrate before the Buddha and Tara. As a messenger of the Buddha the name of Crybaby Tsering became widely known. Everyone came to have faith in the "Crybaby Saint".

He would write down people's complaints before they expressed them to him and then he would have them listen. Everyone would feel ashamed and forget about their complains.

The truth is Tsering was still learning to read and write. He would read and write people's minds and then read it out loud. People would heal their own minds through Tsering.

Tsering became a true *chunzhung* of the temple.

Comment:

The first stupa that I built is in Ladakh. Ladakh is in western Tibet and belongs to the state of Kashmir in India.

It took about ten years to build the stupa. At that time I visited many Tibetan temples and got to know many little monks. Many of them are at an age when they long for their mothers, but remain in the temple and work hard in serving it. It had a deep impact on me and it was distressing when I compared them to the children of modern Japan who lack spirit. It was there that an eight-year-old orphan named Tsering came with some villagers. He just carried his birth certificate in his hand, with a seemingly embarrassed and lonesome face, and stood hiding behind the villagers. From that day onwards he became a little monk in my temple. Inspired by his circumstances and the wonder that he turned out to be, I wrote this story.

Simple Sonam

Simple Sonam was born in a small mountain village in Tibet.

He had grown up physically and in years but his mind stayed more or less the same. His parents knew that his intelligence was not keeping pace with his age. Simple Sonam was able to walk by himself, but whenever he tried to speak he would just laugh foolishly without knowing any words. His parents were so distressed with his delayed development.

His family was poor and they were simple farmers living in a canyon valley with a sliver of land and some cows and sheep. One day his parents went to talk to the Lama in the village temple. A Lama is a Tibetan monk.

The Lama did some fortune-telling using the Tibetan calendar and dice. He recited a sutra and received some offerings from them.

He said, "Sonam is simple, but he was born under the protective star of the Buddha. Take him to town and put him into the temple there. I will write you the letter."

The Lama then wrote the letter to the Lama in town. Sonam's parents took him across the mountains and through the valley. They walked several days and finally arrived at the town temple where they handed over the letter.

There was no hospital for the disabled in this Tibetan town. Everyone would bathe in the sun in front of the temple or walk around it. Even if someone was unwell or disabled, everyone provided them with meals and took care of them so they could live suitably. They became part of the surroundings of the town.

The town Lama took pity on Sonam. He said, "What I can do is just shave his head, put a robe on him and make a place for him to sleep under the stairs in front of the temple. The townspeople will all look after him. It would probably be good for him to walk around the temple."

He then received Sonam from his parents.

Soon the full-moon festival celebrating the Buddha's birthday arrived. Sonam looked like a Lama. He also carried the shrine over his shoulder and walked around the streets.

Everyone sang out loud *Kyi Kyi So So Sanguay Shi Gelong* (May Buddha Live Forever) while marching along. Interestingly, Sonam was able to learn those words and speak them through the strange power and energy of the full moon.

Every day of the year, after the festival, he would put his hands together and sing out loud *Kyi Kyi So So Sanguay Shi Gelong* while strolling around the temple. Simple Sonam also became part of the town's surroundings.

No matter who he met, he would put his hands together and sing out loud *Kyi Kyi So So Sanguay Shi Gelong*. Those people who possessed good sense thought it awkward, but for the people coming from the villages it was delightful. No matter how simple he was, his respect and good wishes for a long life for others were appreciated.

The townspeople discriminated against the villagers. They had a strange smell of rotten butter and frowned a lot. The store owners also overcharged them. But the villagers loved Simple Sonam after being treated terribly by the townspeople.

The kids often threw stones at Simple Sonam and teased him, nevertheless he folded his hands together and laughed his silly laugh shouting *Kyi Kyi So So Sanguay Shi Gelong.*, The kids would give up and carry on playing. Eventually, they invited him to play with them.

For Simple Sonam everyone who gave him food was a Buddha. He really loved walking around the temple, but he would never step foot into the main hall. He instinctively felt he was not meant to go inside and instead just circled around the temple. The Lama taught most of the little monks. He fostered the talents of those children who could study, paint pictures of the Buddha, cook meals or recite

the sutras beautifully, each of whom would walk their own paths. He also felt perhaps the town needed Simple Sonam who would, at the very least, recite *Kyi Kyi So So Sanguay Shi Gelong* while walking around the temple. He was pleased that Simple Sonam had his place.

Sometimes in the market the shopkeepers would argue over the prices with customers. Simple Sonam would then leap up towards them shouting *Kyi Kyi So So Sanguay Shi Gelong* while laughing. The argument was then over and done with.

Sometimes in houses in town there would be arguments between married couples.

Simple Sonam would then come shouting *Kyi Kyi So So Sanguay Shi Gelong* and try to get into the house. The argument was then over and done with.

Sometimes trucks on the narrow road would not give way and a big fight would happen. Simple Sonam would then come shouting *Kyi Kyi So So Sanguay Shi Gelong* and try to open the door to one of the trucks. The argument was then over and done with.

Sonam seemed to have sensed the unique energy coming from people's minds, whenever there was an argument. So as soon as an argument started, he would jump in shouting *Kyi Kyi So So Sanguay Shi Gelong* laughing.

Some of the bad kids would try so hard to teach him foul language, but he just listened grinning. After a brief pause he just shouted *Kyi Kyi So So Sanguay Shi Gelong*! When people were rejoicing in a wedding, or were very sad on a funeral, Sonam would remain hidden. It was only when a fight erupted that he would come shouting his magic words.

As the townspeople had become affectionate towards him, the Lama tried to provide Sonam with a room as it was cold under the stairs during the winter, but he would never enter the main shrine hall. He always stepped back and didn't go into the room.

One year during the winter Tibet was hit by a great wave of cold air and it went down to minus forty in the early morning. Sonam was buried under the snow and was chilled to death below the stairs. His face was calm and smiling.

After Simple Sonam died, the people realized how arguments in town had reduced and how peaceful the place had become thanks to him. They held a great funeral to honour him.

It was then that the Lama of the town temple found in the ancient Tibetan Buddhist scriptures a "teaching of the excellent lotus". He thought perhaps the twentieth bodhisattva mentioned in it might have actually been Simple Sonam. The townspeople never realized that there had actually been a bodhisattva present among them and felt ashamed of their ignorance.

They then started thinking that there might be a bodhisattva present anywhere and at any time in places you'd never notice. Everyone then started folding their hands in respect when they met each other.

Comment:

In this story we see the training of Sadāparibhūta Bodhisattva (the Bodhisattva of Never Despising) from the Lotus Sūtra in Ladakh. As a basis for this story I used the image of a certain Lama I met, who had a disability, how he was accepted by the townspeople and their devotion for him plus my own experiences paying my respects up close.

In today's society people suffering disabilities and learning disorders live their lives differently from us. Social welfare acts, safe environments and well-equipped hospitals and other centres have made things quite accessible and positive for them.

In Tibet there is a lack of hospitals and centres for the disabled. Welfare, which Japanese would consider only natural, does not exist.

However, in ancient history such people were quite insignificant and had no function, but in a religious society they formed a support for the hearts of people — healing others and inviting smiles while contributing in their own ways.

Such qualities are not common in Japan today, so through this story I try to send a message to the children of today. What I hope this story conveys is a sense of personal reflection, as we are always thinking with our heads. I also hope to convey a feeling of true understanding of the fact that pure devotion is the foundation of Buddhist practice.

4

King Yak

There was a yak that lived on the Tibetan plateau. He had big horns and long shaggy hair hanging all the way down to the ground. He was King Yak.

Great people live in high places. That's precisely why King Yak didn't live anywhere else but the Himalayas on the Tibetan plateau, which is called the roof of the world. He was maintaining his prestige of being the king of cows.

Although he was king, he was always alone. Sometimes he was with other yaks, but he preferred to live alone in peace. As he lived in a very high place, the servant cows couldn't come even if wanted to.

The King was a wild yak. Most of his companions had become servants to people and lived with flocks of sheep, though King Yak never became familiar with humans.

That's because while he had his position as king of cows, the idea of "king" is really just a product of human language. Yaks don't have such titles in fact.

Moreover, he didn't live in a stream of time as fast paced as the flies swarming around his tail and back, but nevertheless people lived several times faster. Thus, King Yak couldn't live with people.

One day as always he was chewing on some grass on the green plains of the Tibetan plateau, watching the clouds drift by. He saw a monk with a horse loaded with many books come slowly walking by. Strangely, the books were surrounded by a brilliant glowing light.

This yak was King Yak. He was called king because he was large and strong.

Still, to other beings he never conveyed a sense of being radiant and in need of gratitude.

The King had a strange feeling and approached this monk. This man had come all the way from faraway China and had been to India. He had loaded many sutras onto the horse that recorded the Buddha's teachings and he was on his way back to his hometown now. It was a dangerous journey to go to India from China. He had to cross deserts and follow the Silk Road while cutting through Tibet and climbing over the Himalayas before arriving in India.

After visiting various places in India and collecting many sutras recording the Buddha's teachings he was walking back to his hometown in China. He had finally arrived on the Tibetan plateau.

The horse he had brought with him from India couldn't bear the load on his back any longer. His back was giving up. His energy had sapped and couldn't swallow the rough grass on the plateau, so his health had become poor over the days.

The monk rode the horse on flat land, but when they reached Tibet the horse became weak and he had to walk. The two of them were exhausted and finally collapsed in front of the king of yaks. It was quite difficult for them to adjust to the atmosphere in Tibet where the air is thin at such a high altitude.

King Yak spoke to the horse, "Hey Mr. Horse, what are those glowing things on your back?"

"Mr. Yak—these are the precious teachings of the Buddha that guide human beings. My master collected them with great difficulty. We are returning back to his hometown and he hopes to share them with fellow beings, but I am wasted and cannot move anymore."

The horse closed his eyes and sighed. The next moment he passed away right there.

The monk looked up at the sky and broke into tears. He pulled himself together and then started reciting a sūtra. King Yak fell into a trance listening to his heavenly voice. He dozed off and had a dream. In the dream he saw the Buddha seated smiling in radiant light. A light emerged from between his eyebrows, illuminating the countries far to the north-east.

Tracing the light back to its source, the Buddha was not there, but instead it was the sutras on the back of the horse from which the light was coming.

King Yak then understood why he was where he was today. He realized why he had never become livestock. It was clear that if today he did not carry these sutras then the heavenly light would not reach the countries to the north. He knew in a flash that this was the purpose for which he was born.

King Yak had to take up this mission — to carry both the monk and the sutras on his back to that faraway country.

When the monk finished reciting the sūtra as mourning for his companion horse, the large bundle of sutras on top of the horse's back floated up into the air and came down snugly on the yak's back.

The monk cautiously approached the yak, who then bent a knee and invited him onto his back. Now the journey of the two began.

King Yak was contented because he was not serving humanity, but serving the Buddha. The monk was also satisfied because he couldn't walk any further on the Tibetan plateau.

King Yak knew the plateau like it was his own backyard. He took the flat paths and knew every spring. They never lost track. The journey took many months before they finally arrived in the Chinese capital. King Yak's hair was always black, but carrying the radiant sutras on his back changed his hair into pure white all over.

The emperor of China was quite pleased. He gave great rewards to the monk who had brought back the exceptional and valuable teachings of the Buddha from India.

The monk then built a temple and took on disciples before translating all the sutras into Chinese. Later, the translated sutras made their way across the sea to Japan.

The people adored King Yak. The emperor also assigned some people to take care of him. He was not exploited by people like most beasts of burden. On the contrary, now humans were serving him.

He made people imagine the Silk Road, Tibet and India. He lived a long life cherished by everyone before he passed away.

The emperor and the monk honoured King Yak and used the hair from his tail in rituals daily, waving it back and forth in front of the altar while praying.

Did you know that the horsetail whisk that the monks use in a temple when performing a service is actually yak hair? The sutras that King Yak carried on his back blessed us with a peaceful life. That's why monks wave around horsetail whisks as an offering of cool air to the Buddha every day. Till today this has been used for the Buddha and to welcome good spirits.

The teachings of the Buddha are not just for few people. King Yak risked his life in coming all the way to China. The teachings of the Buddha that we cherish were taken from the plains of India over the Himalayas and then through Tibet across the Silk Road to China, Korea and finally Japan.

The sound as it whirls around is the tune of the souls going round and round.

Comment:

This story made me think how Buddhism might have been brought from India to China by a yak. I wish to express that it was not just humans, such as those great monks of China, who brought Buddhism to China and Japan, but also animals who contributed to spreading it. In China and Japan we know that the monks' whisks are made from yak tail hairs. Young people should visualize how Buddhism spread out across Asia in places like India, the Silk Road, China, Korea and Japan.

5

Kuro

I'm a cockroach called Kuro.

I live hidden in a department store where I run up from the basement to where all the food shops are and go crawling up to the roof, like a free cockroach.

My closest friend and rival is imprisoned on the ninth floor in a pet shop. He's an African beetle and has special status. We call him Beet. My own mother got caught in a cockroach trap and died a martyr's death.

Beet had been abducted from the mountains. Now, while he doesn't have his freedom, they did put a sign saying $3000 in front of his cage and the kids come to look at him affectionately. He's safe inside.

I have my freedom, but whenever people see me, all scream in panic and try to stomp on me.

Beet and I have heated discussions in the middle of the night over the matter of freedom versus special status.

I am jealous of Beet who gets to eat delicious food and is admired by everyone. They say, "Oh, what a fabulous colour!" I have got the same colours, but don't get called anything other than slimy. That's why I often have a fit and take off for the sky.

I'm clumsy and when I fall down right away, people in the store suddenly create uproar and scatter here and there in fear.

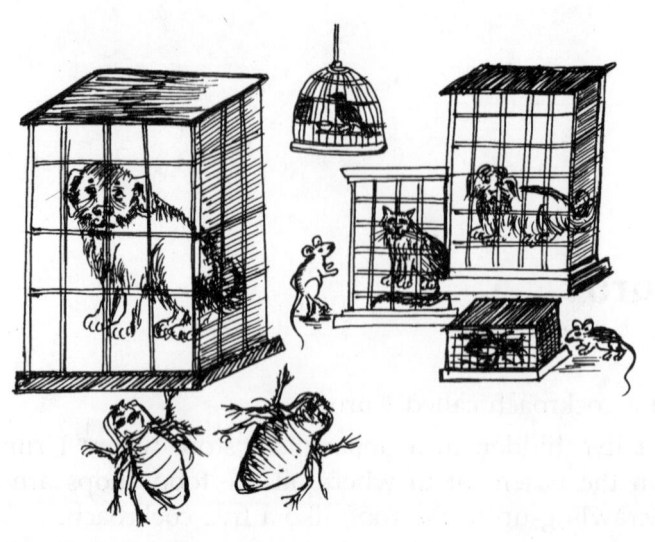

But Beet is also jealous of me because he lives in a cage and has no freedom. At a price of $3000, he should at least receive some of that money yet the shopkeeper takes it all like a slave driver. He could have got hold of that money and got away from the cage.

I try and stress to Beet that freedom is frightening, while he explains to me the tediousness and fears that come with luxury. The discussions late at night are heated. The other insects and rats gather around and listen intently. This is because these discussions reveal a kind of value judgement that exists for us insects and animals.

"Confinement and special status."

"Freedom and discrimination."

"Universal value and relative value."

There are always two sides to every coin.

The rats understand me. The pure bred puppy named Pooch is in favour of Beet.

Here I should formally introduce my new friends.

The rat is Don Brown of the underworld. He calls himself Emperor of the Tokyo Night, but during the daytime he's an untouchable who slinks around the gutters.

I say to him, "What, you don't want me talking about you? Um, we're not the same people—I'm an insect. Insects don't live like mammals. We have a different way of living in the same world."

The rats calculated things according to their own way and formed their own gang to overwhelm the human population with their numbers. Don Brown is one of the gang. He comes up to the ninth floor of the department store. He knows the "game trails".

Pooch is a pure bred dog. He was born high class and confined to be sold like a slave. He's an illegitimate dog born because a human, otherwise called a breeder, impregnated hundreds of female dogs with a male dog. Pooch's only pride in life is his price tag of $8000. He has fun drawing in all the kids and fathers with his puppy eyes. They all stare at him sighing. It was his perverted idea that he could get a master quickly acting like this.

Incidentally, I don't have such a problem—I am my own master and independent. I think it would be definitely interesting if humans could know about our late-night discussions, but the wavelengths are so different that they wouldn't understand. We have a more rooted existence.

Our instincts tell us beforehand when an earthquake will occur. Still, as a law for those knowing their nature, we live bearing our fates and numerous handicaps.

Humans try to drive those of us away who live in tandem with nature. We might then be venerated in a museum of natural history if we go extinct, but roaches and rats who won the population wars are still subject to termination. Pooch's other dog friends are also terminated. Our fate is decided by human value judgements.

One of my friends is the playboy Firefly who is adored by people. There is a song about the "Light of the Firefly", but with the increased use of chemicals on farms his kind are on the verge of extinction. Although he is a pest who shoots fire out his rear, yet people respect him.

I worry about where to draw the line in this issue. I even painted my wings in the cosmetics shop, but they thought I was a jewel beetle. I was turned into a specimen in a collection. In the end a cockroach is still a cockroach.

What really struck me in a flash of insight then was that we will far outlive humans. No matter how awful the environment becomes, humans might go extinct, but cockroaches will stubbornly endure! This was my realization as a cockroach.

Life after life in cyclic existence, it is better to long preserve a species.

Notwithstanding the chemicals used to kill us or the stomping we encounter, we are sure to outlive humans! All said and done, we'll win the battle against discrimination! The rats also agree.

The one thing that concerns me now is that human tastes might change and that roast roach might become popular. I pray that never happens. Of course I don't expect roaches will be cooked as an appetizer anytime soon, but humans are a threat to us.

That's why if some people start eating roasted roach, please single them out and stop them! Cry out if you have any human decency!

Still, those little ones shooing away bugs are cute! Their evil has its limits.

6

The Big Tree

The Big Tree was a rest spot for the villagers in an Indian countryside. During the hot summer it served as a comfortable shade where the villagers would come for afternoon naps. In the evening the villagers would come out of nowhere and gather around the tree chatting about old times.

The Big Tree existed for an unspeakably long time as compared to people. Even if he made friends with people, they were born, raised, aged and dead in a moment's time, which is why the Big Tree always had to experience the sadness of separation.

Still, he could sense life going round and round.

If one of his human friends disappeared, after some days a somehow familiar feeling baby would be born and raised again. In their old age they would come to the Big Tree to talk and the separated friends would be reunited.

So, even if the body was different, it was just their spirit changing forms. It was like the cycle of life. However, people never noticed this. Even if you tried to talk to them about it, it was unclear how to go about discussing it.

There was someone who did understand such things. It was the monk who wandered around the villages with a begging bowl. The villagers didn't know it, but they somehow felt it. Like embracing their mothers they would always gather in the shade of the Big Tree. It would make them feel at ease.

Time passed.

The seasons changed.

The ages changed.

People changed.

But the kindness of the Big Tree never changed.

Staring out into the distance the Big Tree, firmly rooted in the earth, conveyed his kindness to everyone. There was no real need to do so, though he had been nurturing kindness for a long time.

When he saw people busy running around, the Big Tree wanted to comfort them and show his kindness. He had nurtured kindness in people for a long time, so the old people knew real kindness. Still, when humans have come to know kindness, they again have to be reborn. The time when they come to accept life and realize things comes to an end. They would then have to start things over from the beginning. They would move forward and backward, forward and backward.

This is why the Big Tree would sigh.

You should try gently placing your ear on the trunk of the tree. You can hear the whispers and sighs of the Big Tree.

When you reflect on yourself, you can probably hear the whispers of the Big Tree.

Time flows quietly. If you go up that quiet stream, people age while struggling and suffering. Go along with that quiet stream of time. This is the wisdom of old people—the whisper of the Big Tree. Today, too, while flowing in the gentle breeze you can hear the whispers of the Big Tree. The Big Tree always prays that you will be able to hear those whispers before you become old. That prayer is that perhaps you will entrust your body and mind to the long stream of time.

That's why the sutras which the monks recite while begging in the villages come together with the whispers of the Big Tree and echo throughout.

The Big Tree in the Indian countryside still provides shade for the spirits of the villagers and will remain a support for us during our hard days.

Comment:

I wrote this story after seeing how in the Indian countryside villagers would always gather under the Bodhi Tree to nap, talk and drink tea. I wondered just how much time they spent under the tree. When you're in India the trees really seem to live like us and have their own awareness as if they're somehow thinking. It is an awareness that is completely lost in the bustling modern Japanese society.

I hope that people will at some point of time stop and think about this awareness.

Kumari

Kumari was an eight-year-old girl. Her parents had died and she had become a lone orphan at such a small age. She was taken in by a rich household and helped out in the kitchen while living as best she could.

This was in Kathmandu, Nepal.

Kumari was a sweet and innocent girl. She was skinny, had clear eyes and a beautiful face, which always left an indelible imprint on people's minds. People would get choked up when they heard her story.

Kumari would always wear a big jewel around her neck that was a memento from her parents. It wasn't an expensive stone, but was large and turquoise in colour. Nevertheless, for Kumari it was her sole treasure and the most precious gem that she possessed.

One day the town was bustling as people started gathering in the streets. It was that day when an old fortune-teller was going to decide who the goddess would dwell in.

In Kathmandu it was an annual event. The goddess would dwell in a young girl for a year and bring fortune to the people. When the year had passed the girl would go back to being normal again.

Today the girl in whom the goddess was dwelling for the past one year had changed back to being normal, so they were seriously searching for a new goddess.

The previous night the fortune-teller had a dream.

He saw a poor girl, who was thin and had clear eyes. There was a big turquoise stone around her neck and she was working hard in a kitchen of a big house.

In the dream the fortune-teller visited her.

"Where's your mother and father?" he asked her.

The girl replied, "They were called away by the Buddha and went to heaven ahead of me. However, they watch me from heaven, so you don't have to worry about me, sir."

She continued, "Light comes out of this stone and they are always talking to me."

The girl in the dream then faded away.

The old fortune-teller told everyone in town about the dream and ordered them to find the girl quickly.

It didn't matter how big the town was, there were not so many lone girls who wore a large turquoise stone around their neck. Soon, people gathered outside her house. The fortune-teller accompanied them and did not give any reason for his visit to the master of the house. He just requested for a glass of water.

The master quickly called out, "Kumari! Quickly bring this gentleman some water!"

He then guided the fortune-teller into the house.

Kumari came out with a glass of water unaware of what was going on. When she gave the glass of water to the old man, he jumped up and folded his hands before her pressing his head to the ground in respect. She was taken aback. The master was also surprised and didn't understand the reason for this.

The people who saw this started shouting, "The goddess has been found! The goddess has been found!"

They lifted her up and seated her on a ceremonial shrine before flocking into the streets of Kathmandu.

The Himalayan goddess this year had come to inhabit the soul of this lone girl Kumari.

The master of the house was also overjoyed. He was respected by the people in town because the goddess had descended into his house and such blessings had been sent from heaven.

Life changed for Kumari. She was bathed in hot water and painted with turmeric spice. Makeup was applied and she was dressed into beautiful clothes. She became a princess.

The lone and poor girl Kumari had become a goddess in a moment. She was surrounded by people, gifted bouquets and showered with flowers and respect. She was not lonely anymore. Kumari would be the goddess of Kathmandu for the year. She would have to smile and touch the heads of everyone who came offering her blessings.

That night Kumari had a dream. Her mother and father came to her.

Her father said, "Kumari! We're sorry we never gave you anything. That's why we asked the Buddha to use your body for just a year for the goddess to live in it to express our feelings."

Her mother then whispered to her, "Forget yourself and for a year do your best to pray for others. If you do, then for the rest of your life the Buddha will look after you."

The next morning Kumari remembered the dream distinctly. She then firmly resolved to pray for Nepal and the world. At that moment, the turquoise stone necklace around her neck started to glow.

She requested the people around her, "Take me to the biggest Buddha in town!"

The people cried out, "A message from the goddess!" They loaded her onto the ceremonial shrine and took her to the biggest temple.

Kumari paid her respects to the Buddha before taking off her necklace and offering it to the Buddha in memory of her parents. So it flew into the air and fell snugly into the space between the Buddha's eyebrows.

Kumari's body was surrounded by winds and she started whirling around. Her body transformed into a strange form that was neither a boy's nor a girl's, saying to the people, "Poor, rich, smart, evil, male, female, a different people, a different religion—you must offer your most treasured possession to the Buddha and go onto the path of the Buddha."

Kumari then fell down from the air onto the ground with a thump and fainted.

Many people came to visit Kumari every day. In Nepal not having parents and, moreover, being a poor girl was thought to be awful, though Kumari had become a goddess.

People now realized that they had been warned by the Buddha about their own shallow thinking. They understood that it doesn't matter if you are poor and have no parents, or even if you're a little girl, you have to hold the courage to give up yourself and your most treasured possession to walk the path of the Buddha.

Now people would take every word Kumari spoke seriously. People started feeling the innocence of their own childhood when their eyes met her clear eyes and, feeling ashamed, they crouched at her feet.

For the lone Kumari there was an empty feeling in her heart—the absence of her parents created an enormous hollowness inside.

That's why the goddess fit snugly inside her.

All of us have a hollow space somewhere in our hearts. Demons often try and takeover that space in a kind heart.

Everyone has a hollow space in their hearts but they try to forget the loneliness and sadness. They try and push such feelings into the corner of their hearts and avoid getting overwhelmed by them. Demons become overjoyed at the prospect of entering this space.

The truth is the Buddha can also enter the hollow.

That emptiness in your heart should not worry you. If you give your most treasured possession to the Buddha, then the Buddha will sit snugly in that hallow space. His presence will put an end to all miseries of life—loneliness, sadness, greediness—and you will be blessed.

For Kumari, her precious possession was the big green memento—the turquoise necklace from her parents.

What is your most treasured possession?

> **Comment:**
>
> *For writing this story I combined two ideas—one from the "Devadatta" chapter of the* Lotus Sutra *that has a story about a Naga Lady attaining Buddha-hood. The other is the ancient belief in Nepal about a Hindu goddess. Before I became a monk I was in Kathmandu. I was twenty years old when I experienced the Kumari festival, I felt strange. It was odd for me to see people worship a little girl. Undoubtedly, there was a kind of radiance about the girl's pure soul.*
>
> *As a monk I venerated the* Lotus Sūtra *and I felt somehow that the traces of the Naga Lady were present in the Nepalese Kumari. In the modern day, religions are divided into categories. Other religions and schools are made separate from our own, but in India and Nepal the traditions of Buddhism and its traces are sometimes found in places we wouldn't imagine. There are also times in the Indian countryside when some customs are similar to what's written in the sutras, being followed since centuries. I wanted to express that kind of meaning in this story and touch on India, Nepal and Tibet.*

8

Tenzin

Ever since Tenzin was aware of the world he had been alone. He had been taken in by a Tibetan family that had crossed over into India from Tibet.

In fact, while Tenzin was a Tibetan name, he had been born where Shakyamuni Buddha had become enlightened: Bodhgaya. He was *Bihari*.

Interestingly, there were many such children in this small Himalayan town. They spoke Tibetan and though you'd think they were Tibetan, they had dark complexions.

Bihar was terribly poor and children who had no parents were sold in the town. Tenzin had fortunately been taken in by Tibetans and from the age of three raised by them. He was now working as a helping hand in the kitchen. So, while he felt a bit different from other families, he liked noodles more than curry, and spoke Tibetan better than Hindi. He was also more familiar with the Buddha than with Hindu gods. Overall, he was an interesting boy.

Tenzin didn't know his real mother. His present father sold Tibetan accessories on the roadside in town. His present older brother had become a little monk in the temple. His younger brother was still small.. His present older sister, the eldest, and a high school student, sometimes taught him English. Tenzin was a part of the family and the only thing that made him different was the colour of his skin. He had no memories of Bihar. Even if he had any, they might have been unpleasant and he would have tried to forget them.

Tenzin was popular in town because he was more Tibetan than the Tibetan kids. From the time he was small he was always with his grandmother who came from Tibet. She had come to India in her later years, so she didn't understand the local language. She stayed inside most of the time or otherwise took Tenzin to the nearby temple and they would walk around it reciting sutras every day.

Tenzin always accompanied his grandmother, so he learnt things from her that modern Tibetans had forgotten. For the lonely pair the events of their lives had guided their souls. The grandmother had lost her country, friends and irreplaceable history and memories. In the Cultural Revolution she lost her husband. Tenzin had lost the home where he was born and his parents. The two of them were separated by age, but had a strong bond and were friends sharing similar lives.

It was a blessing for Tenzin to be been born in Bodhgaya where Buddha Shakyamuni had become enlightened.

His grandmother's tales were painful and sad. But in the memories of her lost country, there were seven colour rainbows and the blue skies of Tibet. Her memories of youth were bittersweet like apricots and Tenzin loved those stories. In the end she would always finish by saying that how she was able to come to Shakyamuni's homeland and visit Bodhgaya, where she thanked Shakyamuni for having gotten Tenzin.

She was fortunate to come to Bodhgaya at that point in her life, because if such a thing hadn't happened then she definitely wouldn't have had the chance to come to India and visit the holy land of Shakyamuni. She knew the chances of that happening were uncertain no matter how many times you're reborn.

So, although she lost her country, husband and memories, but she saw it as a test from Shakyamuni — she believed it was a gift to make a pilgrimage to the holy land and get Tenzin. It was a support for her heart.

Tenzin's job was to help his mother in the fried noodle shop. He also had to babysit his younger brother. Everyone in town loved Tenzin. It was fun listening to him speak Hindi, the local language. Everyone smiled brightly whenever he spoke Tibetan, shouting to his mother for an order of fried noodles or dumplings. Everyone had some pain in their heart and while slurping their noodles they were comforted seeing Tenzin's tranquil face despite his circumstances and the love he shared with his mother.

Many villagers from deep in the mountain countryside would come into this small Himalayan town for shopping. They were all Indians from the Himalayas, so they enjoyed eating Tibetan food which they couldn't cook themselves. So after shopping they would eat fried noodles and dumplings at Tenzin's shop, which was a small pleasure for the villagers. They would also meet Tenzin there.

That was the scene in this small town in the Himalayas. Different kinds of people gathered together and various religions, languages and customs weaved together into a tapestry. Their hearts flew like a magic carpet.

Tenzin definitely was guided by the Buddha to this small town to comfort the hearts and minds of the people. In the small towns of the Himalayas there are many such youths. I feel that all of us should meet them. . These are towns in the Himalayas where the gods live.

The Little Bird

Part 1 – The Heart's Shell

In a quiet little house in a harbour town there was a little bird who would look to the evening sky out west and feeling uneasy watch the migrating birds fly westward with the changing of the seasons. In her faint memories as a chick she recalled being part of a flock of migrating birds with her mother and father, but had got separated from them. She was rescued by some kind people and looked after by them until now.

Nobody noticed or knew as it was believed she would get big, lay eggs, raise some chicks and spend her life in a warm house while being affectionately cared for by everyone.

Still, as her body got big her blood seemed to roar. She naturally longed to flap her wings in the sky. She would secretly fly nearby when the family was on vacation and the house was empty. It was not as hard as she had expected. There was no strain once she felt the stream of wind under her wings and flew. It became easy.

Such an experience included a strange sense of liberation and bliss, but one false step and it seemed she would be attacked by predators and hunters. She felt an unspeakable hesitation and fear of the cold wind and rain. Before the family returned she went back into her cage.

Her heart was always waving between her wild instincts and her motherly nature to lay eggs and raise chicks. As the cage got smaller, she heard a voice suggesting a bigger home be built. Still, she could hear another voice calling her to soar into the sky, flap her wings to a distant world and meet spring there. The little bird didn't understand any longer how to tackle this new feeling.

Returning to the wild would mean obtaining freedom in exchange for walking a path of thorns.

If she laid eggs and raised her chicks, it would be boring but peaceful.

What did her mother and father want for her?

What did the people around her want for her?

What did her heart want? What was it trying to jump at now?

Where was the place she would return to? Was there such a place?

Her thoughts and feelings and sense of responsibility and gratitude to the people around her were bewildering.

The little bird close to dawn would look up at the stars in the night sky for guidance; she could only hear the sound of the wind and sea. Like a chick which breaks its shell and is born into the world, she hoped to see a day when the shell of her heart would break and she would no longer be the little bird and instead be the migratory bird?

Would that blood and instinct for migration be passed onto her chicks and then their chicks even if she stayed in the little town?

Birds can freely fly the world—the Himalayas, Siberia, the southern Islands, the Eurasian continent and the plains of India. The little bird was always dreaming in her cage of flying around the world.

"Yes—wings have a mind of their own."

Whether she could or couldn't fly around the world, her heart was growing just like her wings that were becoming bigger and bigger. The chirping of the little bird in the cage would also definitely reach those birds in migration and then her mother and father. That voice would echo through the forest and over the sea, comforting and aiding plants, animals and people. It would echo for eternity.

The little bird spent the winter, crouched in her cage. She tolerated the cool draft blowing through the wings of her body and mind, continuing to wait for spring while keeping warm.

Part 2 – Shangri La

The long awaited spring arrived.

The little bird's wings had become a bit bigger and her cage was also made bigger. As her chirping voice had become greater, she had been put out on the balcony of the house.

With her beak and feet she became good at opening and closing the hinge on the cage while playing innocent. Then one day, which felt like an early summer, she finally couldn't take it any longer and in a daze joined a flock of migrating birds. She became part of a formation of migrating birds which were about the same size as her. They crossed the sea and mountains before finally arriving in the place called Shangri La.

There in Shangri La the snow was starting to melt. The plum and apricot trees were in full bloom. The high mountain plants were springing up from between the snow banks and rocks while the water melting off the snow flowed pure. Everything was alive with the breath of spring.

In Shangri La there were still no borders between people, animals and plants. Everyone lived together in harmony.

There were no lights, but at night things would glow with the soul light of beings. At 3000 metres above sea level the night sky on the high plain twinkled as if all the gems in the world had been sprinkled across it.

Part 3 – The Old Garuda

The full moon of May came to this land.

The people there all believed in the Buddha.

Today was the Buddha's birthday and many people brought flowers, incense and many other things from the Himalayas, offering it to the stupa, a monument which housed the Buddha's remains. They threw their whole bodies on the ground in respect and prayed, which the bird watched from up in the sky.

It was then that the Old Garuda, a bird which lived hidden in the Himalayas, came out dazzling in golden light. It was a bird which, according to legend, only appeared in the human world on the full moon day in May. He then paid his respects to the Buddha before shedding soft golden mist over the people visiting there. He flew round and round the blue sky to ensure good fortune for the year. Unfortunately, human eyes couldn't see any of this, but they could somehow feel it. It seemed like the New Year would bring good things.

It somehow felt pure, the heart overflowing with joy. From up in the sky above the little bird intently watched everyone chattering.

During the night of the full moon the stars stopped talking.

The soft moonlight lit up Shangri La and the people started to meditate.

The Old Garuda, who had been flying all afternoon, quietly meditated in the shadow of a rock while his wings glowed bluish-white under the moonlight.

The little bird watched the figure intently. She wanted to ask the Old Garuda, who had been living for so long since ancient times, about her worries. She slowly came close to him.

The Old Garuda opened his eyes slowly and fixed his eyes on the little bird. Before she could chirp anything he started speaking.

"The bird is born after breaking through the egg. It flies around in accord with the movement of the soul. The soul also has a shell, but it is very hard and cannot be shattered open."

"I have prepared a medicine with herbs that are only found near a secret spring deep in the forests of the Himalayas. I will give you this medicine. You will break open the shell of your heart and be able to take a new journey, but it will also include the pain of separation. You will face danger. The Elder Nightingale will tell you when it is time."

"It is by the Buddha's wish that I come to the earth once a year from the world of souls. You must fly to the bright stars before night turns to dawn. All beings carry with them countless worries and pains. This is why there is no time to hear each of them, but put this medicine in a bag and hang it around your chest. Protect it! When the Elder Nightingale's cry can be heard and he tells you now is the time to take it, take it!"

Having spoken, the Old Garuda became unapproachable like a stone statue. The little bird then put the charm around her neck and returned to the little town where you could see the sea, sighing with a feeling of relief. She knew the family had been worried. While happy, she still felt frustrated that she couldn't tell them about her strange experience in Shangri La. She chirped, but the family just saw that she was well and couldn't imagine what she was thinking.

The little bird lost her voice chirping, but finally gave up. She used the wings in her heart to travel around in her dreams. From an outsider's perspective she went back to the same old dull life.

Part 4 – The Elder Nightingale

After having been to Shangri La the little bird hid the charm Old Garuda had given her in her feathers. Now more than ever she was deeply thinking about various things.

The following year spring came. A single elderly nightingale from the forest announced the arrival of spring on the balcony of the quiet house in the small town where you could see the sea. The people in town all knew that spring was coming by the sound of his cry. The plants and animals could all feel the breath of spring in their bodies.

It was then that the little bird recalled what Old Garuda had said would happen. Hearing the cry of the Nightingale she realized what she had to do. The beings called humans were different from the birds. They couldn't chirp. They use all kinds of words we can't understand and are always muttering something or other whenever happy, sad, upset, angry or crying.

Until now the little bird had felt helplessly jealous, but hearing the cry of Elder Nightingale her mind went blank and she somehow understood something different from what she had been feeling until now.

She then timidly went over to Elder Nightingale on the balcony and asked a question.

"Humans use words to convey their feelings to others, but all we can do is chirp. Why is this?" The little bird chirped as best she could.

Elder Nightingale slowly tidied up his wings and closed his eyes.

"When you chirp, you really don't understand if you hear something from the ear, or if it connects directly to the soul, or through the ear it connects to the heart, but when something warm enters the heart it sounds like this.

"Try listening to human words. They get the meaning and they can express their different feelings, but most of the time rather than enchanting and delighting others it angers and disturbs them, or makes them cry and argue. Their use of language is more often than not meaningless."

"We with a single chirp go past meaning and kind of directly reach the soul. We express our feelings to others with various melodies and high, low, quick and slow sounds. At the same time for those people, plants and animals that don't understand the meaning, it sounds like beautiful music as it comforts their hearts."

"This is why it is far greater in meaning than human language and makes people happy."

It was then that the little bird understood why she chirped and dreamt of chirping as best she could in the distant skies, in the forest, over the sea and around humans. What she understood was the mind becoming quiet. When it was quiet, the door to the soul opened up.

Elder Nightingale saw how she looked and said, "The time has come."

He chirped three times and returned to the forest. The little bird, without thinking what was to come, lost herself and took the medicine that was inside the little bag around her neck.

Part 5 - The Stone Door

The little bird felt like electricity was running through her whole body and then fainted.

She dozed off into a dream. Everything in life happened as if it were a dream. She recalled things as if they were on a cinema screen running through her mind. She entered into a new world.

There was a large stone door there. She chirped once and the door suddenly opened. She could then go inside. There all the humans were quietly sitting in and walking around cages suited to their body sizes. There were also people in big cages. There were also people crouched in small cages. There were also wild people swaggering around pens big enough for an elephant to enter. It seemed like they were now all waiting to fly freely like the birds — to look up with longing eyes at her soul and to hear her chirp.

It was then that the little bird realized it: until now she had been raised, cuddled and fed by humans, but in reality it wasn't like that because she and other birds were looking after people from above and comforting them with the sound of their cries. She felt somehow assured.

She then went into the cages of those most lonely and sad, and found herself chirping to help them dream of soul journeys.

Part 6 – The Iron Door

The truth was that little bird was taking care of people.

It was a surprising truth. If people ever noticed, she thought maybe they would never be able to get over it. She felt a bit sad and hurried away. She stood before the door made of iron and chirped once. The door then quickly opened on its own again. Beyond a vast field there lay a sprawling thick jungle.

There were many dancing peacocks with vibrant coloured feathers. One or two tried to run to the field and tried to fly, but strangely fell right back down. They would then run on the ground again. The little bird thought it was quite pitiful how the peacocks would try to fly again and again, but just fall on the ground. In the flock there was the Peacock King who had the most splendid wings. The little bird hesitantly went up to him and worked up the courage to ask a question.

"Why can't the peacocks fly in the sky?"

The peacock king in a loud voice like an angry wild cat cried out. He spreads his dazzling feathers and conveyed a message into the mind of the little bird.

"You have become big and able to see some of the world."

"Living beings have various abilities; they can't have hundreds like the gods. If you have one ability, you must sacrifice another."

"Our ancestors gave up flying for beautiful feathers, but we can dance. On the land there are many frightening beings. We gave up beautiful singing. We now live protecting ourselves with a threatening cry which scares away other animals."

"Our ancestors knew the taste of poisonous snakes and insects. Poison is a flavour that cannot be really described. Once you eat it, you cannot stop. That poison gave us all the more beautiful feathers."

"Little bird, know this well! Once you get something, you must lose something else."

Part 7 - The Bronze Door

The little bird was struck with a truth like it was a sharp knife. She became scared and quickly escaped. She cut across the field and finally stood in front of the third bronze door. Again she chirped once. The door quickly opened again. There was a calm countryside farm. Round chickens were wandering around the garden. The mother hen was in a pen laying eggs, not looking like she was thinking about anything in particular.

From up above she intently looked at the sprawling fields of wheat and rice. The western sky was turning red with the sun setting. Night was coming and the stars were starting to glow. The little bird felt a bit lonely and crawled into a bird box on a big tree to rest.

Before night turned to dawn, the bright stars started shining brightly. When a line of light touched the great tree, the chickens all cried out together. The little bird heard them saying, "Wake up! Wake up!"

The little bird hesitantly went to ask some questions to the one with the finest crest and long tail: the Chicken King.

"Why is it that the chickens don't fly in the sky? Why does the mother hen stay in the pen and just lay eggs, only to be quickly taken by the humans and eaten? Your bodies are turned into kebabs, soup stock and fried chicken. You are lined up on the kitchen tables of humans and eaten, but why don't you escape?"

The Chicken King stared down at the little bird and replied.

"You have gotten bigger and now understand a bit of the world."

"I will tell you. Our ancestors were actually humans. Some of our friends now were humans in past lives. Some will be reborn as humans."

"Even if we lay many eggs and sacrifice our bodies for humans to eat, the nutrition the human gets is great and so the merit means the soul of the chicken will enter the womb of a human mother and be reborn as a human."

"This is why, little bird, we are further from the soul world than your kind, but we live closer to the human world. We satisfy human hunger. Humans instead eat eggs and chicken, and when they do it becomes a part of their body, blood and mind. Sometimes we are reborn as humans, sometimes we return to being chickens and again are eaten."

"But humans are beings quite terrible at awakening the soul. This is why in the holy moment before dawn we cry out and try to wake human souls."

"Still, unfortunately only humans close to the soul really understand. That's why those humans close to the soul wake up early every morning for prayers."

Part 8 – The Silver Door

The little bird remembered hearing prayers from neighbourhood houses, temples and churches a bit far away.

Still, she got the feeling she was going to be eaten by humans, so she quickly cut through the big farm and stood before the fourth silver door. Again she chirped once. The door then again as before quickly opened and there was a sprawling desert. Riding the desert wings she flew around for a while and spotted in the desert valley an old camel with faint breath lying on its side.

There was no water around and the hump on his back was also out of water. He was dried up and it looked like he knew death was coming. His warm eyes were glistening with tears and staring out into the distance while quickly remembering everything that happened in his life as if looking back in rewind.

When he was young, he loved his mother and her milk. He would always hang from her utter and others made fun of him. He also became friends with human children. He would look into the small shops and exhibitions in the bazaar. He was excited by the dances, music and circuses there. He had been a part of a caravan group and had gone to many towns, villages, seaside harbours, the pyramids, big rivers and beautiful oases. He was aware of the proud feeling about the weight and responsibility of carrying cargo on his back when he had grown up and did it for the first time. There was also that warm gaze from his parents watching.

He slowly walked the great earth, over hills and mountains, and through deserts. He would eat small grasses seemingly hidden in various places and carry on walking.

It was such a joy when they found an oasis. The beauty of the glistening water and how pleasant it was on the throat when drinking it! There were times when after a long time in the scorching heat an oasis appeared and he used the last of his strength to get there, only for the mirage to vanish. At night the sky was full of beautiful stars which looked like gems scattered across it. It seemed the stars held hands and formed shapes, which helped ease the mind. If you spoke to the constellations, they would always reply.

The camel really loved the stars making up the Virgo constellation—her sweet whispers and comforting words. When he was bullied or tired, she would rain down light to him.

The next favourite was Pisces which told the best stories.

The thing the camel longed for the most was the pure blue boundless ocean. The Pisces constellation told strange stories about the sea along with letting him listen to the sounds of waves.

Various fishes swam inside it. Seawater was blown up into the air like it was a whale, the largest creature in the sea, spouting water. Sometimes flying fish would get tired of the sea and fly around the sky like birds, but fall down right away. There were also blowfish with prickly spines full of poison just in case a predator came. There were also squids and octopuses with many legs. There were shellfish that recorded the sound of the roaring sea. If you put the shell to your ear, you could hear it even on the ground. There were fashion shows of fish in the red forest of the sea called the coral reef.

The Leo constellation spoke of the jungle. Countless children had shared their stories with the stars, so you never became bored in the long dark nights of the desert. The Milky Way would sometimes flood and make a sound as it flowed. It always made a murmuring sound which put you to sleep.

The camel had been paired with a female and had kids. It was a proud feeling when their kids also started hauling cargo in the caravan. There was also the sadness and empty feeling from when his parents suddenly went away.

The caravan left behind footprints every day, but the wind had only to blow once for them to vanish. As if snickering at the uneasiness of walking a pathless path and the proud feeling of making it on one's own, without any regard for your pride, the wind had only to blow once for all one's hard work to vanish. It was an empty and pitiful feeling when that happened. He recollected various events in life—it was wearisome and bitter, but some sweet tears ran down from his eyes and into his mouth, moistening his throat just a bit.

The old camel was following the law of camels—when you know the time of death has come, you leave the caravan and go to a desert valley away from people where nobody can see, and then die there. You sudden become aware of the law when you realize you'll die. He also came to understand the reason why his parents suddenly left. He was quietly breathing when the sky started to rumble.

They had sharp beaks and claws. There were dozens of vultures starting to circle in the sky.

They sensed the smell of death, and came as the messengers of the underworld. They anticipated what was coming.

Again, while he was gasping for breath and still breathing, a couple of the flock came down to the ground as if drooling and, approaching the camel, started poking at his rear with their beaks.

The camel had been in a trance looking back over his life until now when suddenly he returned to reality where he sadly realized he was nothing more than food for the vultures. He sighed and died right there. At the same time dozens of vultures swarmed down onto the corpse and devoured it, head to tail, in a way so viscous you wouldn't think it was of this world.

The grey-feathered vultures completely hid the camel's corpse. In not even an hour only a white skeleton remained in the white desert valley. The vultures were stuffed but kept eating, so they couldn't fly away into the sky. They all started their afternoon nap.

Part 9 - Guard of the Soul Country

It was first time in her life that the little bird had seen such a shocking thing as this.

She strongly resented her bird companions who had acted like a gang. She worked up all her strength to approach the Vulture King who was taking an afternoon nap.

"Why did you do such a terrible thing? Why did you not at least let him die slowly?"

The Vulture King glanced at the little bird and looked away, but pulled himself together and looked back.

"You've gotten bigger and come to be able to see the world well."

"I didn't turn my head away just not, little bird, because I dislike you. We vultures actually only ever speak to those returning to the Soul Country. Everyone calls that "death" but really we tell those people headed there that the time has come by circling around them in the sky."

"But, little bird, to know the truth is to lose something."

"I know the truth, but if we speak any more, then you might lose something important. This is why you should quickly leave here!"

The Vulture King quickly turned aside.

The little bird didn't feel so good. She had watched a frightening thing happen, or rather how could anyone be at ease with this sort of thing? What was this Soul World?

She really wanted to know and couldn't stand it. Even though he said she would lose something important, if she was able to know it for real, then she could become more and more of an adult. A key moment like this would definitely only come maybe once or twice. She recalled in Shangri La the form of the Old Garuda and what she felt. She pulled together her courage and went behind the Vulture King and chirped, asking to be told the truth.

The Vulture King made a serious face and turned away, but closed his eyes and giving it some thought asked a question.

"Little bird, were your parents migrating birds? Now where are you? Why did you come to the entrance of this dark world?"

The little bird, chirping, did her best to explain how she had come this far.

King Vulture's expression suddenly changed and he looked welcoming. It felt like the faces of her mother and father were overlapping and smiling. He was beaming with compassion and replied, "Little bird, you've done well coming here. Now you can get the transit visa from King Yama the customs officer."

"Life is short when it seems long. It is long when it seems short. Again, even if you return to the Soul Country, you must come back here right away. More importantly, I should tell you the truth. Looking at how much time you spent, to send you back now would mean you wasted your effort after getting through the silver door. So I will tell you."

The Vulture King then wrapped the little bird in his wings as like a cloak. It was as if he was going to sing a nursery rhyme. He whispered it in a way that was pleasant to the ear.

The little bird thought of Bodhisattvas about whom humans sometimes talked about, which were like this. Though this Vulture King should have been frightening, listening to what he said was a sweet and bitter feeling like when going to bed at night you don't know if you're awake or asleep.

Part 10 – Preparing the Heart

"When body and soul become one you are born on this earth. The new body for the soul is created based on one's personality and past life actions. This is why in this world there are various forms of animals, reptiles, insects, fishes and plants. It's just a short trip, we're here on earth for a while working, playing, and doing both good and bad deeds before we return to the Soul Country. That's why everyone's homeland is the Soul Country."

"It is brilliant there—there are no forms like people, animals and plants. Everyone is a ball of light flying around while living, mingling and healing together. Sometimes they are born in this world. When they are born they live within the body that the earth provides before returning to the Soul Country again."

"This is why a body without a soul should be eaten soon so it is useful to other beings and doesn't rot. This is why, in order to tell beings of their return to the Soul Country, we feed right away so they don't have attachment to this world and so the souls don't get lost on the earth or in the dark tunnel to the Soul Country."

"Some people, like the old first worshippers of the desert and the Tibetans, would feed corpses to vultures. Christians and Muslims will bury them in the soil and let the insects eat them. It fertilizes the soil and plants grow there. Buddhists and Hindus burn the corpses right away like they would light incense to offer to the divine."

"It might seem cruel to you, little bird, but you eat little bugs which dream of becoming butterflies flying around the sky. Don't you eat the wheat and rice that tries so hard to live from spring, which lets you fly? You haven't noticed, but you are the same as us."

"You are more frightening than vultures for the little bugs which become butterflies. That's because you eat them though they dream of living and flying. You never think of telling them that they will go to the Soul Country—you just snap them up at once."

"In that respect, we vultures have a sense of responsibility and awareness of our role as messengers of the Soul Country. We circle above those who are going to die."

"There is an important secret behind the circle. It's neither a triangle nor square. It's a perfect circle. The earth is round. The moon is round. The soul is sound. The truth is round. Eventually the time to understand all this will come."

The Vulture King closed his eyes and seemed to make a decision.

He continued, "Little bird, you must soon be reborn on the earth because only the transit visa was issued."

"So, little bird, I will give you a mission to do on earth. It has become a troubled time there. You have come this far and close to the truth. You can definitely manage, I think. It is important that you are reborn on earth with this mission."

The vulture then started speaking quietly.

Part 11 – Vision of the Dharma King

"Humans are thousands of times more frightening than vultures. They fight wars and kill millions of people. It might be excused if it was to eat, but out of hatred and pleasure people kill people. They kill many more beings beyond what they need to satisfy their appetites. For their own convenience they destroy nature, burn forests, kill plants and steal the homes of animals. They pollute the air with gas. They kill the fish by polluting the rivers and seas. They are trying to kill the whole planet; really humans are the cruel ones as even the vultures shake in fear because of them."

"Little bird, the human population now is rising like a flood. The time when they will eat up all beings is near."

"Do you know why humans are increasing in number? Humans steal the homes of animals and kill them while forcing them into the Soul Country, so there is no place for them to be reborn and they can only come back as humans."

"So people nowadays just do silly things. They fly in the sky, go underwater, cut through the desert in jeeps, drive cars as big as elephants and carry a lot of cargo. They sing like they were chirping all day long. They can see far with radar like bats do. With big machines they can do telepathy, which is something we have from birth, to talk to and shout at others around the world."

"This is because they have memories and instincts leftover from their past lives. So, somehow, it seems familiar to them. They're drawn to these things and run around all day."

"Little bird, you won't be reborn on earth as a migrating bird again. The forests have become few and the air is polluted. To the humans you are called 'a protected near-extinct bird' — you just live in zoos and in library books."

"So, you've made connections with the people who helped you and the kids who loved you. You've flown around the world and made friends with the people of Shangri La. You'll definitely be reborn as human. There is no other way. Now you must save those humans trying to kill the planet and themselves. I am already old and it was the Buddha's wish that I stay here at the gate to the Soul World as a guard."

"Little bird, I shall give to you a message for saving this world, just like when long ago there were passenger pigeons."

"When you are reborn as a human, realize your mission to save the planet. You will ask the Buddha to help you get the right parents, country, body and time period for this. Do not worry. Now leave here!"

"You will forget your mission because of the pain you will experience when reborn. When you do remember it, it will be a bit bitter. Still, without that shock the human mind and body will not really remember such things. As the Chicken King said, humans really are beings terrible at waking the soul."

He went back to being the Dharma King and, ignoring the little bird, returned to his job as guardian of the soul country.

Part 12 – The Golden Door

The little bird, wrapped in warm wings, couldn't understand each word as if it was sent from mind to mind.

She then noticed, understood, knew, felt and realized something real. She had feelings of bliss and found herself then standing before a sparkling golden door.

She strangely recalled the Elder Nightingale who had announced the arrival of spring. From her beak she naturally chirped out loud. The glittering golden door then slowly opened.

This chirping was the magic word which could open the last door.

A round tunnel extended onward with a single beam of light shining from within. The little bird was sucked through the tunnel at high speed like a rocket towards the light. While being sucked through the tunnel her wings, feet and body disappeared. She noticed, just as the Vulture King had said, that she had become a ball of light.

She plunged towards the light at the end of the tunnel.

Part 13 – The Soul Country

The figure of the Buddha suddenly appeared in the dazzling light, around which countless balls of light glowed. The little bird was moved and lost in feelings of bliss.

Looking to her left and right, her mother and father were watching her smiling.

For the little bird, who had turned into a ball of light, being a little bird was nothing more than a distant memory now.

Light twinkled as if saying, "I am back!"

It felt like her parents said, "Welcome back!"

As they were light, they had no beaks and couldn't chirp. There was no need to really speak. They could have a conversation with the twinkling of light.

She could hear her parents' conversation.

She heard her father say, "When we went to the earth as migrating birds we lost this child and were worried. It was great that some nice people helped and raised her, but a wild animal can't be kept as a pet by people. They're different from dogs, cats and chickens. Still, it is great that we could finally see each other. I don't know where we will be reborn next, but we can't have another lost child."

She heard her mother say, "I was oh so worried, but this is a real good child serving her parents who takes on a mission from the Dharma King and by the grace of the Buddha will be reborn as a human to save the world. We should go ahead of her to earth and make a home that's good for this mission."

The two balls of light then became shooting stars and disappeared into the horizon.

The ball of light, which was the little bird, felt grateful that she could see and meet her parents again and be born from them once more. It was with deep emotion that tears of light twinkled as she felt the compassion of the Buddha.

Part 14 – Recollecting the Little Bird

The soul, which was the little bird, tried to remember being a little bird, but it was light now, and before being a little bird it was human, and before that it was a fish and cow. As it start recollecting everything, the past, present and future all melted together.

The past, present and future all existed at the same time. It was a twinkling of light.

She suddenly saw the earth below. The last stage of the bird was to forget all memories of having been a little bird. She used all her energies to transform her memories into light which she sent down to earth.

The man who had helped her returned home late at night to their quiet home in a town where you could see the sea. The rest of the family was fast asleep. In the cage the little bird had become too cold and fell over on her side. The ball of light could see the man was holding her in his hands, staring down at her.

Although from up above the earth is so brilliant, from down below you just see a clear night. In the daytime when there is sunlight you still can't see the world of souls.

The ball of light, which was the little bird, realized that although it is a brilliant world, humans can only see the night sky.

But hints were left for humans: the constellations above in the stars and various forms on earth are revealed to people to have them imagine the world of souls. It is just small children, old people facing death and those praying who can communicate with the world of souls.

Although it was a bit irritating, everyone ends up here and then they return back to earth, so at the same time they would understand and other times they would forget.

The man carrying the remains of the little bird walked the street at night to the coast and stood at the end of the pier, sighing. "The kids really loved you. They'll probably be sad when I say you died. Tomorrow I need to tell them that you joined a flock of migrating birds and headed out west."

"Leaving while so little, they'll probably worry that some other animal would eat you."

Still, it really was a cute bird and he felt a bit upset. If people found out he cried over the little bird dying, he would become a laughing stock among everyone at work and his friends. The man realized he was a part of the adult world that had lost its innocence. Still, he was really sad and his eyes became wet. He tried not to cry and looked up at the night sky.

It was then from the fog of the white Milky Way above a star shone brightly into the eyes of the man and softly dried away his tears before slipping back into the night sky. The man was surprised and looking downward the tears from before were gone. With strange mixed feelings he set the little bird's remains on the waves of the sea and pressed his palms together which he had seldom ever done before.

Listening to the sound of the waves he walked along the pier. He thought to himself about what just happened. He was an adult, but wanted to cry when this little bird died. Looking up at the night sky his tears were dried away and it felt as if he had been wrapped in light.

No, he thought, he had been busy lately and was tired. He was just feeling under the weather. But maybe this experience was to become something really important. Still, if he said anything about it to others, they would probably laugh at him. Again he looked up at the night sky. It was then that a rain of light from the stars poured down onto him. Something warm found its way into his soul in the depths of his heart. He was filled with a strange sense of power. He promised himself that he would try his best tomorrow. Walking along the long pier he returned back along the road to his quiet home in a small town where you could see the harbour.

> **Comment:**
>
> *This story is a bit long. In this story I share the idea of a wandering soul in a little bird's body. As written in many ancient books, it was known that when a being dies the soul takes a journey from the first seven days up to forty-nine or a hundred days. However, children nowadays have no way of reading about this and it would be considered difficult and frightening. I thought maybe by reading this story they could imagine the path the soul takes. I tried to express the difficult concept of rebirth in a story form.*

10

The Donkey's Pilgrimage

Part 1 – Gada the Donkey

Bihar is the poorest state in India, but there are many Viharas (temples) there because it was where the Buddha attained enlightenment and spent much of his life. Bihar gets its name from the word Vihara. It was there that a donkey named Gada was born.

Gada in Hindi means donkey, so really he was a nameless donkey. When people from Bihar use bad language they say *gada* as a curse. When they are upset or feel that the other person is useless, they call the person a *gada*.

Gada was born to parents who carried stuff in a village on the Ganges River. The village was actually close to the river. During the rainy season the river became like a vast sea. Floods would submerge everything and only the tops of some trees here and there could be seen. During the summer season when water dried up it became a vast field and everyone hurried to build small houses where they grew wheat and rice before harvesting it. Gada was in the fields for eight months and then the other four months, during the rains, he lived with the poor family on the train platform where he did various jobs like carrying stuff and collecting food scraps.

Donkeys are shy beings, but when they cry they have the saddest and also the most unpleasant voice in the world. We may feel that he sounds to be in dreadful pain complaining about the many hardships in life.

While they might have soft and shy eyes, they still carry stuff as people command. It is only in really rough times like when they can't move an inch or they are being beaten with a whip that they cry out and remind people of their pain.

Gada was supposed to live many thousands of lifetimes as a donkey, but one day when walking along the train platform he met a monk on pilgrimage from a land far away across the sea, who gave him a rice cracker. The monk petted him on the head and the donkey came into contact with his robes and the beads around his wrist. From that moment he became a "thinking donkey".

For donkeys, thinking was not only useless, but also very dangerous. They might start wondering why they have to carry so much stuff and end up getting whipped. But as a little donkey Gada did not know such things and he treaded through a world of ignorance.

The farmers of the Ganges River lived on the natural blessings from the Himalayas. The mountains provided rich soil on their fields on which they farmed. That's why during the rainy season they fled into the train station and lived on blessings from people. They spent their lives in a way where the blessings of nature and people were the same and they just sought "blessings".

The soft round eyes of Gada from his childhood watched the workings of Bihar, people, beings and nature. His thoughts were like the slow current of the Ganges River.

Part 2 – The Platform

The city of Patna was where King Ashoka lived in ancient times. It is now the capital of Bihar state and a noisy place that seems to be full of contradiction. The platform in Patna station where Gada worked was also a housing platform for people.

The platform didn't belong to anyone, but as if by a strange magic the platform could be turned into anything people wanted. It could become a bedroom if you slept there. It could become a kitchen if you cooked there. It could also be a toilet if you did your business squatting over the tracks. Nobody objected if someone came and went. It was a rent free home for all.

Recently steam-powered trains had gone out of use and there were no more jobs where Gada would carry coal. Gada's owner for work had started carrying stuff around the station just like Gada.

Gada was given to the owner's son Krishna and he carried firewood and vegetables. When rich foreigners were in the station he would take his sisters to go receive blessings from them, so Gada got some free time.

While he had freedom, he had to exchange it in order to go look for food scraps. The cost of freedom is always great. While he really did know the rules of society, he was more satisfied with looking for food scraps freely as a way of studying society rather than getting fed and having to carry things. Gada really liked the plates made from banana leaves that were dropped on the platform. Unlike hay, they were covered in spices, leftover rice and curry. Such flavours made him dream of distant lands, their food, seas, mountains and all the people, beings and nature there.

Sometimes his master would come and tie him up. When that happened he could just snack on nearby scraps. At first he would cry out and moan about his misfortune, but after watching humans passing by he could see that they too were tied up in their own ideas of having to be a certain way or do something because it was their job somewhere. Human eyes couldn't see it, but humans too were all tied up in things not so different from the ropes which tied up the donkey. Unfortunately they didn't notice.

Gada came to realize that being tied to empty things and caught in spells was far worse than being tied up with ropes. He stopped crying and tried as much as possible to avoid being smacked. He also tried to stay close to Krishna.

Part 3 – Krishna

Krishna, an only son, was a carefree youth with big round eyes. Just like he was taking various things from the fields, river or jungle, even in the station he didn't mind at all receiving "blessings" from people that were not "natural blessings". For him they were all the same from the start.

Whenever Gada watched humans he thought how interesting they were as beings because while they thought everyone should be equal, they were still fine with not being equal.

Krishna had his own way of categorizing people who gave him blessings based on their shape, size, language, smell and attitude, and thought of them as different species. So, he had no sense of feeling beneath others, nor did he have any ideas of discrimination. The foreigners were charmed by his carefree smile and gave him "blessings". Their hearts healed seeing Krishna's face and through their generosity they made right their own contradictions and those of the world.

Krishna's dream was to see the sea and go to the Himalayas and touch the snow. There was nobody around him who had seen the sea or touched snow.

A relative, Uncle Brandy, had gone to work in Mumbai and had seen the sea, but had some awful experiences and whenever Krishna asked him about it he just said, "Mumbai is a sea—people drown in it! That's why they say it is on the sea!" He had turned to alcohol and one day he went off somewhere never to be seen again. But Krishna, was sure about seeing the sea and touching snow. He promised himself that he would do these two things.

Krishna believed that money going from the rich to the poor was only natural, like water flowing from the river to the sea. As a little donkey Gada had eaten a rice cracker from a foreign country and was able to think, so he was also able to really understand the minds of foreigners.

Looking at the people from Bihar struggling in poverty was awful, but he understood the feeling of being saved by Krishna's smile when people came all the way here after struggling with their own spiritual poverty and heavy burdens. Gada spent the rainy season on the platform without feeling bored as he closely watched the strange habits of humans.

Part 4 - The Other Side of the Ganges

When the rainy season came to an end, the water level of the Ganges River slowly went down leaving behind fertile soil. The dry river bed started to appear. The family quickly put together a small house with straw laid down for a roof before moving in. For Krishna now it was the goddess of the Ganges River who was giving blessings.

Here and there water remained. The fish that hadn't gone with the river jumped around in puddles. Krishna and his family returned to the wild. They quickly grabbed all the fish and had a curry fish party in the house, which his mother had been waiting for. Today his mother worked up the courage to buy a large amount of cooking oil in an old jam jar she had picked up in the station. Normally a small medicine bottle of oil was enough, but today was a celebration for the new house.

Krishna's father carried stuff like a donkey. He could guide people to their reserved seats with amazing skill. He also developed a skill of placing luggage under the seats when other customers hadn't boarded. He was able to make more money than people would have expected.

Today was a special dinner because it was deep-fried fish in a curry sauce. Krishna's mother had a simple dream where in Krishna's wedding she would buy a large jar of cooking oil and treat the villagers to fried bread. She had always looked up at the grocery store owner feeling embarrassed because she only bought a single portion of oil in a small jar. She was so ashamed that she covered her face with her sari and quickly returned home.

Their life for now was spent in the middle of the Ganges River. There were no electricity polls nor roads, but there was actually a large bridge above them with cars and trucks driving over it. It was really high up — as high as an office tower! The people running over it never noticed that Krishna's family were down below.

Come evening it was a meal celebrating the new house under an oil lamp. Back at the platform the two parents were shy people, but here they were the masters though they had just built a lone little shack in a large field. Outside the sky was full of stars. The lights from the town on the opposite bank of the river sparkled. The Hindus called the side of the river where Krishna's house was at "the other side". It was believed that the dead would go there. On the opposite side of the river there was a town, but over here it was another world with wide open fields.

The children still didn't have a sense of flavours, but they did know that their mother's special fish curry, which was a blessing from nature, was far better than the meals they received from people.

Under the stars Gada looked out towards the opposite side of the river and wanted to tell everyone that humans were living here on this land where the dead were supposed to go. He could just cry out in that direction, but nobody heard him.

Part 5 – The Three Daughters

Day after day the family tilled the vast land. They borrowed a water buffalo and ploughed the fields before planting seeds. The family loaded firewood, bananas and vegetables onto Gada's back which he carried to the market.

The father of the family worried that his three daughters would need a lot of dowry money to get married. Here in India it was a ritual that when a daughter was married her family had to give dowry (money and/or property) to her husband when they got married.

The three daughters didn't know about this and just lived happily on the blessings of nature and their parents. The mother and father carried this burden with them.

The youngest daughter of the family Sheeta was the only one who recognized that Gada could talk. Usha the eldest was too busy to notice. Whenever Gada was in the house Sheeta would play with him. They were too poor to buy toys, but she did get one toy which not even the richest kids could get their hands on. It understood human language and was also big and friendly. Sheeta would always pat Gada's soft head and back and talk to him, just like the girls in town stroked their dolls. The rest of the family would beat him with a whip. It was only Sheeta who comforted him. Her words were still clumsy, but she was the only one who spoke to him. After becoming a more or less thinking donkey able to understand human language he was really hurt by the whips and poor treatment he received from humans. It was just Sheeta who understood this and sympathized with them. Although he was her toy, she became his mother.

The middle daughter's name was Maneka. Her job was to collect firewood that had drifted down from the Himalayas along the Ganges River. She would also mix together the dung from water buffaloes with some straw to make discs which she dried. They would use these for fuel when cooking. That's why she always had to see the ground like a plate. With such a talent she was able to find various things and money at the station platform. She was most proud of having found a wristwatch.

Someone had probably jumped into a train and the strap broke off. She quickly found it shining under the platform and placed it in her pocket. She got her uncle to fix it and then would always have it on her wrist. She also had the job of telling the time to the family. Her father had tried several times to take the watch away from her, but since he could never buy any toys for her and since it was her watch, he gave up and let her keep it.

Everyone thought it was a strange watch because it ran without having to wind it up. They didn't know what kind of watch it was and couldn't figure it out. The band had been torn off from the watch, but it said "Constellation" on it, which was actually a very expensive brand. It ticked away as it was covered in cow dung and soaked in water, yet it never broke. Just as the constellations above told the seasons, this little Constellation told the time to the family.

The eldest daughter was Usha. She had to babysit Sheeta and make meals.

The mother of the family had to work in the field. When they really needed money she would have to do temporary work in road construction with her husband. The mother also taught her Usha how to remove stones and bits of garbage from the rice and beans. She also taught how to grind spices and make flat breads. Apart from serving meals Usha was also responsible for the kitchen, though it wasn't exactly a kitchen—the little house just had a small empty space. There was just a small stove on the right side of the entryway which was the kitchen.

Everyday Usha would also mix cow dung with water and smear the floor with it. It was a way of putting the little house in clean order to keep the bugs out.

Usha always looked forward to her father coming home after having loaded Gada with rice and vegetables. She also really looked forward to her mother coming back with spices tucked into her sari or sometimes bringing back a small jar filled with cooking oil. That's because for the weeks after planting they had no vegetables to eat. They would chop up some raw onions and mix it together with chilli peppers and salt and eat it with flat breads. This was the only stuff they had with them to eat and it continued like this for a while. Although it was clean, it was still quite different from the meals they enjoyed on the station platform. It was a blessing to have vegetables on the table after several days. Until then Usha just had to think smartly to make everyone satisfied.

Usha felt that Krishna taking the two younger sisters out begging on the platform was embarrassing and she could just never do it.

That's maybe why Usha was the one most at peace.

Still, she loved getting blessings from nature. She would collect triangle-shaped fruits from the nearby ponds. She would run up the trees to pluck green bananas and collect nuts. Sometimes she helped milk cows and received a bit of milk in return. She did her best to get food for her family.

Gada now could eat a lot of fresh grass. Humans had such complex ways of getting and preparing food, but there was a lot for Gada to eat right away around him. Here the grass was a blessing from the Ganges River, so the dreams he got from eating it were different from the plates made from leaves back at the station platform. It made him dream of the Himalayas, the green fields of Punjab and forests.

While being petted Gada would think of the fate of the three daughters and become sad. They would work tooth and nail to earn a living. Their beauty would burn out in a moment like a shooting star. Soon they would have children and again be covered in dirt. They would grow old working tirelessly to raise their children. It was a tough life. Gada looked out to the evening sky and neighing loud and hard he cried over the suffering of human life.

Part 6 – Crazy Sadhu

This year everyone was talking about how the Crazy Sadhu, a really strange yogi, who had come to the village closest to Krishna's little house.

Krishna's family were of the lowest caste, so they couldn't live in the village and had to build their small house on the edge of the dry river before moving back to the station platform when the rainy season started. Recently times had changed and such people were now able to get work in the villages where the locals would speak to them, but they continued to live on the dry riverbed.

The Crazy Sadhu was supposed to have had a nice life in the city, but went through a shocking experience which messed up his mind. Sometimes he would twitch, but somehow he looked like a yogi searching for something as he went around all the holy sites of Shakyamuni Buddha. Sometimes he would be given offerings from foreign pilgrims. The villagers in the countryside would always make strange sense of his words. They would look forward to hearing about these holy places which they hadn't and definitely wouldn't be able to go to. They also thanked God that they weren't like the sadhu. Their feelings of gratitude were expressed in meals offered to Crazy Sadhu.

They didn't know why his mind was messed up, but when people see what they weren't supposed to see, they cannot carry on living as usual. Crazy Sadhu had also seen a world he wasn't supposed to have seen. He could only throw himself at the mercy of Shakyamuni Buddha and went on a pilgrimage as if being pulled.

One day, Krishna and his father had delivered the village vegetables and bananas to a truck waiting at the state border when returning back they saw that Crazy Sadhu was surrounded by the villagers, so they went to have a closer look.

Crazy Sadhu shouted loudly while looking out into the distance. "I rode the cloud and went to Thailand, Tibet, Japan, Sri Lanka and China!" "Shakyamuni Buddha was everywhere. Big and small. Sometimes his face is different. Some were outside, some were inside, but they're all from India!" he continued.

People figured that he had visited the temples of various countries at the Buddhist holy sites in India and his mind had travelled around the world.

Krishna and his father pulled Gada along. Just as they timidly came in front of Crazy Sadhu he met eyes with Gada.

Gada thought, "Oops!" and pulled back. It had only been Sheeta who had known he was a thinking donkey, but now Crazy Sadhu knew.

"Master donkey!" he shouted. Crazy Sadhu shoved the villagers aside and threw himself before Gada with palms together.

The villagers thought that it was another of the Sadhu's fits and they all went on with their daily works. But Krishna and his father were simply stunned. Crazy Sadhu was worshipping Gada and reciting something.

When Crazy Sadhu finally calmed down, he said to Krishna's father, "I have met the master I've been searching for many years. I must bring my master to the holy sites. Please give me the donkey!" He then dumped all the money from his dirty purse on the ground.

Krishna's father noticed that there was a green crumpled bill in the pile. He could see that a "100" was written on it. During the rainy season when he had carried some bags for a foreigner, he received a bill with "1" written on it. He had been at a loss what to do with it, but a hippy backpacker exchanged it for 40 rupees. In his head he quickly calculated it at 4000 rupees.

His dream for the longest time was to be able to buy a water buffalo calf. He wouldn't have to spend so much money on renting a water buffalo to plough the fields. On top of that they could get milk and live better than ever, he thought. He couldn't care less about Gada. He just replied, "I can get this changed!"

Crazy Sadhu was overjoyed that he could now exchange this crumpled up piece of paper for his master. For the longest time he could never use it, though sometimes he would smell it to imagine foreign countries. Now he traded it for his master.

Part 7 – The Sadness of Separation

Krishna was simply stunned. He couldn't object to his father. He also couldn't think of any reason to object.

He thought maybe he could have more fun if he didn't have to look after Gada, but he would still have to look after a water buffalo calf which didn't understand anything. Krishna didn't know this and perhaps this was best.

Krishna's father held onto the "100" bill tightly and placed his hand on Krishna's shoulder.

"This bill is going to get us a water buffalo!" said his father proudly. "But for Sheeta, keep this a secret! We'll say Gada ran off somewhere."

Without looking back they quickly went back home. That night Sheeta cried through the night. Her irreplaceable friend had abandoned her and ran off. Krishna's father then came to understand just how much Sheeta had loved Gada. At the same time he realized in himself that when Sheeta the youngest daughter had been born he had grown cold towards her and never gave her so much affection. He started to think that his kids are all irreplaceable. Now he became a good father to Sheeta. That was the parting gift for Sheeta from Gada.

That night Gada also cried over Sheeta, but Crazy Sadhu ignored that and continued chanting his magic words. Gada then felt a sense of ease as if Sheeta was petting him. He had become independent of his mother and was progressing towards his young adulthood, step by step.

Gada noticed that listening to the mantra he went from "thinking" to "contemplating". He cried out one last time towards to Sheeta's small shack on the side of the Ganges River and slept thinking about the importance of love that he had received from Sheeta.

Part 8 – The Start of the Pilgrimage

The next morning Crazy Sadhu quickly put a big string of beads and yellow robe around Gada, though he still made him carry everything. Instead of using a whip he would tap the ground with a stick using various signals to go, stop and rest.

In India there are many people who travel with animals. Most of them have a monkey on the shoulder or a snake around the body. They might find a cow with a hump and put beautiful clothes on it, thinking it a messenger of god and travelling with it. But it was very rare to see some sadhu walking along with a donkey as guru.

Gada as a young donkey had touched a string of beads and robe, but now he was wrapped in them and it felt strange. It was just as if he had left his parents and home to become a monk. He didn't really understand what becoming a monk meant, but although it was faint he felt in the chanting of the sadhu a kind of comfort. He thought, perhaps, his heart had moved on from Sheeta's affection and that was partly because he was going to become a monk.

On the road Gada examined the Sadhu closely. Human soul stays in the body and goes round and round. If it leaves the body then they die. But Crazy Sadhu's soul was not going round and round, but instead would move everywhere and sometimes fly out of the body, which he would forget about before it would happen again.

Gada knew that humans called this a "mental illness". He couldn't talk to Crazy Sadhu like he could with Sheeta. Crazy Sadhu looked at Gada as if he was a god and wanted to get guidance from him. Crazy Sadhu thought of Gada as the only being in the world who would understand his sadness and show him the way plus help him carry the heavy burdens of life. Aside from having to carry stuff, Gada started feeling he had become great and capable of thinking for himself.

Part 9 – Vaishali

Gada and Crazy Sadhu had started walking together and arrived at the first holy site of the Buddha, the village of Vaishali.

The Buddha had often come to Vaishali. It was a big city and birthplace of democracy long ago. It was here that the Monkey King offered the Buddha some honey.

Long ago there were no strict lines between humans and animals like we have now. While shapes, languages and habits differed, everyone lived together in peace. Now it was just humans who were in charge of everything. Vaishali's history had been buried and the Monkey King no longer offered honey to people.

This was the place that the Buddha announced his passing from the world. It was like an elephant in its last days: he looked back and headed out for his last trip.

Gada and Crazy Sadhu passed through here and like donkeys they looked back and cried out before heading north.

Part 10 – Lumbini

They walked along the road for a long time and arrived at the second holy site of Lumbini, where Shakyamuni Buddha was born. Along the way they had to pass the Indian-Nepal border, which didn't seem like much of a border, though a strict looking guard stood there. Seeing Crazy Sadhu and Gada coming along he rolled his eyes and went back inside the office pretending they didn't exist.

Gada thought how odd it was that the guard thought they didn't exist despite the fact that they really did exist, though this guard really believed this border existed. It was then that he became a donkey capable of even more thought.

Right after the rainy season in Lumbini there were flowers everywhere and cool winds blew down from the Himalayas with various birds and butterflies flying around.

Gada knew that Shakyamuni Buddha's mother had seen a white elephant in a dream and became pregnant afterwards. He recalled the story about the Buddha leaving Vaishali behind like an elephant in its last days. He felt envious of this elephant. He thought what if she had dreamt of a donkey instead? It wouldn't have even been a joke, but might have been thought of as an insult instead. It was then that for the first time he could laugh at himself.

Crazy Sadhu saw that Gada was laughing and was so surprised he almost jumped. All the laughter in public had created a wall in his heart and he didn't let people get close. He thought maybe he had seen through it. He hardly raised his head towards Gada. It was under the Ashoka Tree that Prince Gautama was born. He took seven steps and promised to save the world. Later he became the enlightened Shakyamuni. Crazy Sadhu also tapped the ground seven times and promised he would somehow take Gada to all eight of the Buddhist holy sites.

Crazy Sadhu then realized there were eight. Finally he tapped his head with his stick.

"Seven and one are eight!" he jokingly laughed at Gada.

It was then that Gada and Crazy Sadhu really understood each other from the heart.

Part 11 – Shila Vasti

The third holy site was Shila Vasti, which is where the Buddha Shakyamuni had quietly spent the rainy season. It was here that Angulimala the murderer had promised a demon that he would kill 100 people. He had killed 99 people and taken their fingers to put on a string around his neck. He had tried to kill Shakyamuni as the 100th victim, but he was struck by the light of the Buddha and he confessed all his evil deeds before becoming a disciple.

Nowadays, there are more terrible murders happening than what Angulimala had done. There are disastrous things like bombs, mines and machine guns. People are using them mindlessly and killing each other inhumanly. The pollution destroying the environment is an act of murder against the whole planet, but nobody knows when, where and who should express regret about it.

Gada realized that the crimes you couldn't see, rather than the ones you could see, were far worse. This scared him.

Here in the evening you could hear the bells ringing. Crazy Sadhu gathered the pilgrims together and showed them Gada. With the donkey's sad looking eyes and the sound of bells he could get his plate filled with money.

Gada suddenly felt sad and cried out. This had an effect on the pilgrims and the two got more money for food.

Part 12 – Sankasiya

The sound of bells in Shila Vasti and Gada's crying really worked. They got more money than they thought they would. Crazy Sadhu bought two train tickers and tried to get on the train, but just as they were getting in the conductors came laughing and led Gada into the cargo space right at the back of the train before shutting the door on him.

Crazy Sadhu muttered to himself while returning to his seat.

Gandhi, who led India to independence, had studied to become a lawyer in London while young and had a job in South Africa. When he first arrived in South Africa he had bought a first-class ticket for the train and just as he tried to get on board, the White train conductor pulled him down and made him ride in the third-class carriage, which was like cargo space. This was an act of racism and discrimination.

Gada never went to school because he was a donkey, so he couldn't study modern Indian history, but he did feel quite upset and sad.

His mind suddenly felt stronger as the sound of the train on the rails became louder. His mind and body were lifted up into heaven above. His mother and father were standing there. He had been separated from them when he was little. Gada let everything out and talked about everything that had happened until now.

In heaven his mother and father were able to think unlike when they were simple donkeys on earth.

His father said, "Son, you made it! But you can't stay long! If you visit all eight holy sites of Shakyamuni Buddha, then we will be reborn as humans, and then you will be reborn from your mother as human!"

His mother, in tears, said, "We were so worried when you were sold to a poor family! Sometimes we would pet you through Sheeta, or whisper to you through mantras. Did you know? No matter what, you are our irreplaceable child, so take care and finish your journey!"

Gada was lost in his dream hearing this and suddenly heard a *whap* sound before falling into a field of yellow mustard plants.

It was the fourth Buddhist holy site: Sankasiya.

In order to teach his parents Shakyamuni Buddha climbed into heaven and Sankasiya is where he landed when coming back down. The Buddha had climbed into heaven to teach his parents the Dharma, but Gada's parents had cautioned and comforted him.

Gada through of all the holy sites they visited so far, this was the most desolate with almost nothing around. Humans might have believed in Shakyamuni Buddha's teachings, but they ignored and tried not to see or think about the Monkey King offering honey or the Buddha landing in Sankasiya. What they did believe in were just the teachings which fit in with what's now called "modern common sense".

In front of the desolate small shrine in Sankasiya with nothing around he could just cry out for his parents.

Part 13 - Life in the Train

This time Crazy Sadhu himself put Gada into the dusty brown-coloured car at the back of the train and they started their trip to Gorakhpur.

Inside the train Crazy Sadhu started shaking the bells on the top of his stick to receive money from people. The trains in India can be like mini-circuses. There are boys doing headstands, girls doing somersaults, blind singers with beautiful voices, old people plucking violins with only two strings, dancers parading around to the sound of drums and sadhus with snakes and moneys. During the afternoon there's no time to get bored. It is always hard when you get to your station because of so much activity.

Before the train even stops the luggage carrier jump onto the train and try to snatch whatever they can from the passengers and end up arguing with each other. Afterwards there would be all kinds of people with baskets on their heads, selling fruits, peanuts and pastries. Then boys would come in one after another to clean the floors. There would be people seeing their friends and family off. With every passenger there would often be a dozen more people from the village come to wish them well.

Next would be the boys selling sweet milk tea. They don't use disposable plastic or even paper cups. They used disposable clay cups. Having tea made from water like what you find in the Ganges River and pleasant smell of earth is an extreme enjoyable experience. While the tea was being served, beggars would be sticking their arms in through the windows.

During the night the train became a sleeper and those without reservations were chased out, but during the daytime you were free to sit anywhere. Healthy people would sit on the top bunk and shower down peanut shells below. People sitting below just accepted without objecting.

Everyone in the same carriage was family. If someone else had a newspaper or magazine, it was just as much your own. Your own book also belonged to everyone else and if you were not careful it might be passed around and end up in another carriage.

It is also a disaster for anyone wearing a watch. People grab your arm to look at the time. They just want to see what time it is, so your arm is not at all important.

But people will in fact notice you if you have a nice watch and ask you dozen questions curiously.

"How much was it?

"Where did you buy it?"

"How much would you sell it for?"

It isn't all so bad. During the day time the families who brought their lunches share it with everyone. Other people buy their lunches. Everyone tries to be nice and shares tea and fruits with each other, so it becomes a full course meal.

When people move they don't use a truck. They bring everything with them on the train, so there is a lot of cargo—futons, buckets, pots, axes, plates, cups, boxes of clothes and furniture all move with them. The platform might be a home to many, but the inside of the train is also a home. Anywhere can be home, so you can't really be homeless.

Although Gada was in the dark cargo carriage, he could still hear the noise from the passengers. It was like a lullaby and before long he was asleep.

Part 14 - Kushinagar

Kushinagar was the fifth holy site. Here Shakyamuni Buddha passed away under trees with two trunks. When the Buddha died the mice were the first of the animals to come. As they arrived on the backs of cows they jumped off and cut through the crowd of people. They all cried in front of Shakyamuni Buddha.

The cows were the saints of the animal world, so they knew ahead of time that Shakyamuni Buddha was going to pass away, but they were in a hurry, so they didn't notice the mice clinging to their backs. But then as saints they wouldn't have otherwise noticed.

Next were the tigers. The tigers were the kings of the jungle, so they came on behalf of the jungle. Next came the rabbits known for their quick feet. They came running through the grasses crying with red eyes. After that the dragons came. The dragons were in charge of the weather and would make it rain, but they left work in a hurry and came rushing down from the sky.

Then there were the snakes. The snakes were the guards of the gods. The gods started talking about the Buddha maybe passing away, and the snakes got word of this and came swimming down the river.

Later the horses came. When Shakyamuni was a prince running from the palace he rode a white horse called Kantaka. Later it was heard he attained enlightenment and the horses became students of the Buddha.

Next came the goats. They had to come down from the mountain as a group, so it took them a bit of time to arrive. The monkeys came next. They could jump from tree to tree in the jungle, but they couldn't manage so well on the grassy plains, so they were late. After that the birds came. The king of the birds was a migrating swan. He had to wait for the winds to change and rode the jet stream, flying down from the Himalayas. Next were the dogs. They sniffed out the Buddha's tracks and followed them. The last were the wild pigs. Their legs were short, so it was very hard for them. Everyone was out of breath and but they came to say their last goodbyes.

Gada knew about the relationships between people and animals. Gada was disappointed, though, that the donkeys weren't there, but his fellow students the horses did come and Gada felt okay because donkeys are not so different from horses.

Humans had forgotten about the relationships they had with animals long ago, but there is still proof that it existed because in the Asian calendars you see twelve animals, which were the ones that came running to Shakyamuni when he passed away. But those animals and animals nowadays are ignored and Gada under the two-trunk trees in Kushinagar cried out to try and tell people the truth, but the local farmers told him to shut up and threw rocks at him.

It was then that Gada realized what the word "martyr" meant.

Part 15 – Sarnath

Sarnath was the sixth holy site. It was where Shakyamuni Buddha first taught the Dharma. It was actually not humans who first came to hear it, but some deer. That's why now the place is called Deer Park. Everyone knows about it as a kind of fairy tale, but they don't really believe it. Gada really wanted to know when it was that humans and animals stopped talking to each other. Today our kindness and attention towards animals has lessened.

In the villages of India the cow is a member of the family. For travelling sadhus their monkeys are their partners. For those looking after elephants and camels they might think they're in charge, but really they're just looking after the animals.

Gada had found a partner and he was thankful that instead of a whip he just used a stick. Shakyamuni's teachings were difficult for Gada and he didn't understand, but he saw some light in the fact that it was not humans that first noticed the Buddha's enlightenment, but a deer, so he cried out his thanks to the deer.

Part 16 – Varanasi

Varanasi is on the banks of the Ganges River. For Indians it is the holiest place in the world. They divide life into four parts: being a student, living a family life, living in the forest and then finally wandering. When someone finally passes away they meet their end and return to the Ganges River.

Crazy Sadhu got excited as he entered the city. It seemed he was about to have a spasm attack again.

Everyone eventually comes to Varanasi. Gada had been living out in the countryside until now except for living on the station platform, so he was so surprised he took a step back and wouldn't move an inch. Crazy Sadhu finally gave up trying to pull him and went diving into the Ganges River.

Gada slowly opened his eyes and started to look at what was going on around him. There were all these people covered in flowers on top of piles of firewood with people standing around praying and burning them. Close to the burnt bodies there were dogs and vultures loitering around wanting to eat them. Standing around also were beggars without arms and legs, rich people, poor people, old people, kids and foreigners. Everyone was watching or bathing in the Ganges River.

In the middle of the river he could also see bodies set on top of boats and sunk in the water.

It was a frightening scene, but everyone looked satisfied like they were standing before the gates of heaven. Gada understood why. But even for a thinking donkey it was a shocking experience.

The snow of the Himalayas melts into water which becomes the Ganges River which flows to Varanasi, which would then bless Krishna's family with rich soil for growing food before returning to the sea and becoming a cloud and then raining down on the Himalayas.

Gada also came to know how the stream of souls is like the Ganges River in that it goes round and round. Just as the earth has rivers, the stream of souls runs atop the Ganges and returns to the sea of souls before becoming a cloud of souls. It then becomes the rain of souls, pouring down. It then becomes the mountains of souls and the earth of souls before again becoming the stream of souls. Gada took half a step and realized he had come to a return point, he cried out to the other side of the Ganges River, but the people bathing were lost in their own bliss and nothing changed.

Part 17 – Lost Property

Again the rainy season arrived and Krishna's family escaped to Patna Station.

One day Maneka found a small black notebook with something inside it. She looked inside and found a passport.

Maneka was disappointed that there was no money inside, but there was a photo of a southern-looking monk who her father had carried luggage for. The monk had given a big tip and his face was just like the photo, so she rushed out of the station and showed it to her father. He said this was just terrible, so he ran out of the station with Maneka to the bus stop.

The southern-looking monk in yellow robes was still there. He was sitting on top of a pile of luggage, waiting for the bus to Bodhgaya. Maneka and her father were gasping for air and handed the monk his passport. It was so terrible, a pickpocket had cut open his bag with a shaving razor and all the money was gone, but the passport was maybe worthless to him, so he had tossed it on the platform and ran off. The monk was almost in tears. He was far away from home and all his money was gone. He didn't even have the money for the bus to Bodhgaya.

He had so much luggage and no friends. If he walked it was over a 100 kilometres. He could only hold his head in his hands.

Maneka's father felt a bit ashamed thinking about how his son and daughters had received blessings from people up until now and felt he should repay it somehow. He knew that he received tips from people and that it allowed him and his family to make it through the rainy season, but he never realized he had never given anything to anyone.

He thought maybe now was the time in his otherwise hopeless life that he could make an offering to a monk. Now was the time in his life when he needed money the most. He took out the 100 dollar bill tucked in his clothes and gave it to the monk to cover the bus fare and meals.

The monk thought this man was like a messenger from heaven. He had thought this poor baggage carrier had been a bit annoying. Although he had given him a lot of money to get rid of him, the monk now was the object of pity. He realized that as a monk he was mistaken about people.

He then got back his passport from the little girl. He looked into her glittering eyes and thought he should express his thanks while they were still together. Although he tried to say it out loud, the father and daughter didn't understand what he was saying and just mistakenly thought he was reciting a sutra as thanks for the gift of money before putting his palms together in thanks to god's grace.

Maneka had never had so much respect for her father. She wanted to tell everyone about him. She understood that giving blessings was much better than receiving them. She regretted that she had lost out a little by always receiving things and never giving.

Part 18 – Returning Favours

The monk from the south returned to his temple and suffered a second shock when he discovered that the temple caretaker and his family had stolen everything from the temple, including the furniture, and disappeared. There was now nobody around to clean the temple or prepare meals.

The monk felt depressed for two or three days, but then suddenly in the morning when doing his practice he remembered Maneka, that girl with glowing eyes. He also remembered he hadn't repaid them the 100 dollar bill yet.

He thought, "Yeah, I can invite that family here and send the kids to school!" He started feeling better.

He quickly made his way to Patna Station with a friend. Maneka's father was stunned when this monk and his well-dressed gentleman suddenly showed up and speaking politely to him offered to give him a job, a beautiful room and his children a proper education.

His whole family sat behind him worried that their fate was on the line now. Opportunity was knocking on their door. If they didn't take it up then the family could expect to live as they always did—not knowing anything and just living eight months on the river and four months on the station platform.

Maneka's father made up his mind as he knew his children would love to go to school. When he was a child the village teacher only taught him numbers and how to write his own name. Just by being able to read numbers he was able to find seats when carrying luggage. Just by being able to read "100" he knew he could change his donkey to a water buffalo. He really knew how important it was to be able to read.

The family then quickly said goodbye to the idea of getting a water buffalo. They packed up all their pots, bedding, buckets, aluminium plates, cups and everything else. Maneka's mother realized how poor they were and felt ashamed of it.

Krishna was very happy. It was the first time he could ride in a jeep. He would always ride on the roof of the bus as it was a third cheaper. That's why Krishna drew a line between those on the top and those below. Those people below were in another world, he thought.

In the temple Krishna's father looked after the flowers in the garden. At night he kept watch over the gate. Usha and her mother did the cooking and cleaning in the temple. Usha also went to sewing classes and learnt how to mend the monk's robes. Krishna went to school in the morning and in the afternoon he would be a guide in the shrine hall while looking after shoes. Maneka cleaned the temple in the morning and then in the afternoon had classes at school. Sheeta joined kindergarten and later helped Krishna with looking after shoes. The temple had many boxes of old clothes which were donated. They smelt a bit like the south and were kind of old, but they were still beautiful clothes from a foreign country.

Krishna's mother didn't wear anything at all besides her sari, but everyone else wore the clothes from the south and became like different people. She might have kept wearing the same sari, but stopped covering her face with it out of shame. She started looking at people in the eyes. She also became able to laugh at times.

Part 19 - Life in the Temple

In the temple Krishna's father learnt how to fertilize and water the garden. On the side of the Ganges River you never had to use your head because things would just grow naturally without watering or fertilizer, but here he had to pay attention. He thought about how up until now he had relied on blessings, but now he was really independent.

Krishna's mother had to make meals for the monk and guests. She learnt how to properly prepare meals and serve it on nice dinnerware. She was also taught how to make all kinds of food from the south and west for the monks visiting on pilgrimage. She also stopped serving tea with her thumb in the cup, and how to have meals at a table rather than on the ground. Over time her downwards gaze turned upwards and she started to show her original beautiful glow. She learnt how to keep things clean, nice and tasty.

There was always a stock of plenty of spices and cooking oil. She knew her simple dream of being able to buy cooking oil in a big can had come true. She didn't use a lot of oil and spice, which was appreciated by everyone in the temple as it meant simple and natural flavours. She realized her way of living up until now hadn't been mistaken at all. She came to have self-confidence.

Usha was taught how to pick the flowers her father planted and put them into a vase as an offering to Shakyamuni Buddha. It was also her job when meals were ready to offer a portion to the statue of Shakyamuni

Buddha. Usha would never receive anything when living on the station platform, so making offerings to the Buddha was an ideal job for her. She also learnt how to put her palms together and pray. Just like a caterpillar becomes a butterfly, she started to have a kind of radiant glow.

Krishna became the quickest when learning anything at school. His discipline hadn't come from Bodhgaya, but from Patna Station. He also really liked looking after the shoes and being a guide in the main shrine hall. When visitors tried to give money, he would point to the donation box. He liked being able to tell them that they could put the money in there. He wasn't hungry anymore, and he also got to wear nice clothes, so he felt more happy being greeted by others rather than receiving spare change. He started feeling happy that people admired him.

Maneka didn't need to look down all the time as if she was looking for something. Now she looked straight ahead and could now see different things. The world suddenly got ten times bigger. She couldn't pick things up, but now she could pick up knowledge. Still, she always left the floor shining like a mirror when she cleaned.

Sheeta started going to kindergarten. Nobody ever bought her a doll to play with, but the people on pilgrimage adored her and put her in different types of clothes. She became like a doll with changeable clothes. She was also able to speak the language of the south country.

Part 20 – Bodhgaya

Gada had no appetite for days and wasn't eating anything. Seeing what he had seen at the Ganges River had been a bit of a shock. He wasn't drinking water or taking any food. Crazy Sadhu's spasms also hadn't stopped since Varanasi. He gave all his money to the roadside beggars. He was flat broke, so he couldn't buy any food.

The two of them arrived at the stupa of the seventh holy site of the Buddha: Bodhgaya. Gada felt heavy as a rock and couldn't move any longer. Crazy Sadhu left Gada behind for a bit to go begging.

It was then that Sheeta on her way to kindergarten found an exhausted donkey.

Sheeta's environment had changed so much that she had forgotten about Gada, but she did remember the day her father had suddenly become a nice and a real father to her. It had left a deep mark in her mind. Gada was surprised to find Sheeta here. Seeing her he knew that Krishna's family had found good fortune and were now living well.

Gada was about to cry when he remembered how Sheeta would comfort him. She looked into his eyes and feeling bitter sweet love gave him the lunch her mother had prepared. She then suddenly had a painful feeling of remembering something she couldn't put her finger on, and turned around before running off.

As Gada's tears hit the ground the shock of the Ganges River also left his heart. As he ate Sheeta's lunch he also felt his strength return. Earlier he couldn't move because he was just too tired, but now he was sitting completely still in meditation.

Crazy Sadhu also managed to get some food and went back to Gada. Seeing that his master was sitting in such deep meditation he thought he had definitely made the right choice in selecting him as his master.

When the morning star at dawn gave off the last of its light, Gada felt something warm rise up in the depths of his heart and he attained enlightenment as a donkey. It was the highest level of thinking a donkey could get to.

It was the knowledge: "I am a donkey."

After Gada had become able to think, he had forgotten himself, denied it and that's why until now he was burdened with so much confusion, worry and pain.

But donkeys are not supposed to carry pain; they are just supposed to carry stuff on their backs. Gada came to realize this. Early in the morning under the Bodhi Tree where the Buddha attained enlightenment Gada cried out and surprised all the people visiting.

Part 21 – Rajgir

Rajgir was the eighth and last holy site of the Buddha that Gada and Crazy Sadhu were to visit.

Gada faintly felt that they were getting close to the end of their trip, but after seeing Sheeta and knowing that Krishna's family was doing well he didn't have to worry any longer and could relax.

It was a three-day trip from Bodhgaya to Rajgir, but along the way they got older step by step and by the time they arrived at the gate into Rajgir they were old and wrinkled.

When Gada was young he would watch the slow stream of the Ganges River. He remembered how time had seemed to stop. In the period of three days it felt like time had rolled on like a wheel. Now he realized that time was not fixed and that it didn't always stick to the clock and calendar. The clock and calendar were just pointers. He came to understand that the real stream of time was different for various peoples, animals and plants.

As evening approached they could see Vulture's Peak, which was shaped like the wing of an eagle. In the dimness of the evening they went up the mountain.

This was where Shakyamuni had spent the last eight years of his life. The two of them were utterly exhausted and collapsed like logs at the top of the mountain.

During the night the two of them seemingly soared into the sky full of stars above and could suddenly see as if it were in the daylight a pure white stupa decorated in gems. They could see a smiling Shakyamuni Buddha at the front of it. It was then that the two of them looking at each other realized they had spent their lives treated either as a donkey or a crazy person.

Gada had been a monk in his past life. He used to talk a lot and say good things, but his behaviour wasn't so good.

That's why in this life he was born as a shy donkey, but he had trained as a monk before so when he came into contact with the robes and monk's beads he could spend his life as a thinking donkey.

The two of them were now happy and chuckled. Gada wasn't a donkey anymore and Crazy Sadhu wasn't crazy anymore. Sadhu's soul was as usual quite well, but without the confines of a body he was free to move about.

When Sadhu had been visiting the holy site of Bodhgaya and all the temples of foreigners there, his mind would always wander to those foreign countries. No matter what, he wanted to go back to Bodhgaya. He made a request to Shakyamuni Buddha where with a smiling nod Sadhu became a shooting star and found his way into the belly of Krishna's mother.

Gada remembered what his parents had told him in Sankasiya. When he visited the Buddha his mother and father became shooting stars and vanished into the eastern sea to be born in the distant land in the east. Until they were adults and could meet again before coming together and getting married, Gada would stay and carry stuff.

What kind of stuff? The stuff that people carry with them in life.

Here at Vulture's Peak the visitors carry with them the heavy burdens of life. They bring them to the feet of Shakyamuni Buddha. It was Gada's job now to take such burdens away.

He wasn't a donkey anymore, but his past life experience as one had been useful.

The next morning the monk who had given Gada a rice biscuit at Patna Station many years ago came up to Vulture's Peak for morning prayers. He noticed the two sets of beads and robes on the dead donkey and man, and thought how strange as he stared at them. As a ray of light appeared the bodies vanished and only the beads and robes remained.

He vowed to the Buddha to be as bright as the morning sun. His karma became lighter and lighter before disappearing with the sound of donkey steps in the distance.

His step also became lighter as he headed to the stupa of King Ashoka, climbing up through the jungle.

That was the first duty of Gada.

It was also Gada's way of returning the favour of the rice biscuit.

Comment:

This is the longest story in this book.

In this story I tried to combine an introduction to the eight holy sites of the Buddha and the Buddha's own history along with some imagery of India's poor. I did this largely from the perspective of a donkey, which is normally considered a pitiful animal. In the end I wanted to present the holy site of the Lotus Sutra: *Vulture's Peak.*

In this way young people can become familiar with the holy sites of Buddhism and realize that India, along with its image of poverty and pollution, is actually warm and alive with nature.

It is my hope that someday these young people might have the good fortune to visit these holy places in India.

THE STERLING BOOK OF...

The socio-cultural realms of society have been explored here. The essence of Indian dances, religions and philosophy has been encapsulated in these books interestingly.

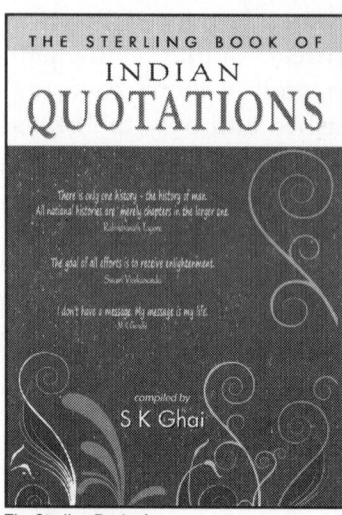

The Sterling Book of
Indian Quotations
S K Ghai
978 81 207 7161 1 ₹ 99

Unity in Diversity
O.P. Ghai
978 81 207 3739 ₹ 99

Ramana Maharishi
M. Sivaramkrishna
978 81 207 3788 4 ₹ 99

Essence of Indian Thought
Baldeo Sahai
978 81 207 5348 8 ₹150

Buddha and His Teachings
Kingsley Heendeniya
1 8455 7 168 9 ₹ 99

Essence of Sufism
978 81 207 5694 ₹ 150

Qur'an
O.P. Ghai
978 81 207 6154 4 ₹ 99

Hinduism
Dr Karan Singh
978 81 207 5585 7 ₹ 99

Bhagavad Gita
O P Ghai
1 84557 426 0 ₹ 99

Indian Classical Dance
Shovana Narayan
1 84557 169 6 ₹ 99

Ma Sarada
Prof M Sivaramkrishna
1 84557 203 7 ₹ 99

*for complete Catalogue
visit*
www.sterlingpublishers.com